One last steep ridge of the rough, boulder-strewn road lay between the royal party and the descent into Velalisier Plain. Valentine, who was leading the way, rode up over it and came to a halt, looking down with amazement into the valley. The land that lay before him seemed to have undergone a bewildering transformation since his last visit. "Look there," the Pontifex said, bemused. "This place is always full of surprises, and here is ours."

The broad, shallow bowl of the arid plain spread out below them. From this vantage point, a little way east of the entrance to the archaeological site, they should easily have been able to see a huge field of sand-swept ruins. There had been a mighty city here once, that notorious Shapeshifter city where, in ancient times, so much dark history had been enacted, such monstrous sacrilege and blasphemy. But -- surely it was just an illusion? -- the sprawling zone of fallen buildings at the center of the plain was almost completely hidden now by a wondrous rippling body of water, pale pink along its rim and pearly gray at its middle: a great lake where no lake ever had been.

Evidently the other members of the royal party saw it, too. But did they understand that it was simply a trick? Some fleeting combination of sunlight and dusty haze and the stifling midday heat must have created a momentary mirage above dead Velalisier, so that it seemed as if a sizable lagoon, of all improbable things, had sprung up in the midst of this harsh desert to engulf the dead city.

It began just a short distance beyond their vantage point and extended as far as the distant gray-blue wall of great stone monoliths that marked the city's western boundary. Nothing of Velalisier could be seen. None of the shattered and time-worn temples and palaces and basilicas, nor the red basalt blocks of the arena, the great expanses of blue stone that had been the sacrificial platforms, the tents of the archaeologists who had been at work here at Valentine's behest since late last year. Only the six steep and narrow pyramids that were the tallest surviving structures of the prehistoric Metamorph capital were visible -- their tips, at least, jutting out of the gray heart of the ostensible lake, like a line of daggers fixed point-upward in its depths.

"Magic," murmured Tunigorn, the oldest of Valentine's boyhood friends, who held the post now of Minister of External Affairs at the Pontifical court. He drew a holy symbol in the air. Tunigorn had grown very superstitious, here in his later years.

"I think not," said Valentine, smiling. "Just an oddity of the light, I'd say."

And, just as though the Pontifex had conjured it up with some counter-magic of his own, a lusty gust of wind came up from the north and swiftly peeled the haze away. The lake went with it, vanishing like the phantom it had been. Valentine and his companions found themselves now beneath a bare and merciless iron-blue sky, gazing down at the true Velalisier -- that immense dreary field of stony rubble, that barren and incoherent tumble of dun-colored fragments and drab, threadbare shards lying in gritty beds of wind-strewn sand, which was all that remained of the abandoned Metamorph metropolis of long ago.

"Well, now," said Tunigorn, "perhaps you were right, majesty. Magic or no, though, I liked it better the other way. It was a pretty lake, and these are ugly stones."

"There's nothing here to like at all, one way or another," said Duke Nascimonte of Ebersinul. He had come all the way from his great estate on the far side of the Labyrinth to take part in this expedition. "This is a sorry place and always has been. If I were Pontifex in your stead, your majesty, I'd throw a dam across the River Glayge and send a raging torrent this way, that would bury this accursed city and its whole history of abominations under two miles of water for all time to come."

Some part of Valentine could almost see the merit of that. It was easy enough to believe that the somber spells of antiquity still hovered here, that this was a territory where ominous enchantments held sway.

But, of course, Valentine could hardly take Nascimonte's suggestion seriously. "Drown the Metamorphs' sacred city, yes! By all means, let's do that," he said lightly. "Very fine diplomacy, Nascimonte. What a splendid way of furthering harmony between the races that would be!"

3

Nascimonte, a lean and hard-bitten man of eighty years, with keen sapphire eyes that blazed like fiery gems in his broad, furrowed forehead, said pleasantly, "Your words tell us what we already know, majesty: that it's just as well for the world that you are Pontifex, not I. I lack your benign and merciful nature -- especially, I must say, when it comes to the filthy Shapeshifters. I know you love them and would bring them up out of their degradation. But to me, Valentine, they are vermin and nothing but vermin. Dangerous vermin at that."

"Hush," said Valentine. He was still smiling, but he let a little annoyance show as well. "The Rebellion's long over. It's high time we put these old hatreds to rest forever."

Nascimonte's only response was a shrug.

Valentine turned away, looking again toward the ruins. Greater mysteries than that mirage awaited them down there. An event as grim and terrible as anything out of Velalisier's doleful past had lately occurred in this city of long-dead stones: a murder, no less.

Violent death at another's hands was no common thing on Majipoor. It was to investigate that murder that Valentine and his friends had journeyed to ancient Velalisier this day. "Come," he said. "Let's be on our way."

He spurred his mount forward, and the others followed him down the stony road into the haunted city.

The ruins appeared much less dismal at close range than they had on either of Valentine's previous two visits. This winter's rains must have been heavier than usual, for wildflowers were blooming everywhere amidst the dark, dingy waste of ashen dunes and overturned building-blocks. They dappled the gray gloominess with startling little bursts of yellow and red and blue and white that were almost musical in their emphatic effect. A host of fragile bright-winged kelebekkos flitted about amongst the blossoms, sipping at their nectar, and multitudes of tiny gnat-like ferushas moved about in thick swarms, forming broad, misty patches in the air that glistened like silvery dust.

But more was happening here than the unfolding of flowers and the dancing of insects. As he made his descent into Velalisier, Valentine's imagination began to teem suddenly with strangenesses, fantasies, marvels. It seemed to him that inexplicable flickers of sorcery and wonder were arising just beyond the periphery of his vision. Sprites and visitations, singing wordlessly to him of Majipoor's infinite past, drifted upward from the broken edge-tilted slabs and capered temptingly about him, leaping to and fro over the porous, limy soil of the site's surface with frantic energy. A subtle shimmer of delicate jade-green iridescence that had not been apparent at a distance rose above everything, tinting the air: some effect of the hot noontime light striking a luminescent mineral in the rocks, he supposed. It was a wondrous sight all the same, whatever its cause.

These unexpected touches of beauty lifted the Pontifex's mood. Which, ever since the news had reached him the week before of the savage and perplexing death of the distinguished Metamorph archaeologist Huukaminaan amidst these very ruins, had been uncharacteristically bleak. Valentine had had such high hopes for the work that was being done here to uncover and restore the old Shapeshifter capital: and this murder had stained everything.

The tents of his archaeologists came into view now, lofty ones gaily woven from broad strips of green, maroon, and scarlet cloth, billowing atop a low, sandy plateau in the distance. Some of the excavators themselves, he saw, were riding toward him down the long rock-ribbed avenues on fat plodding mounts: about half a dozen of them, with chief archaeologist Magadone Sambisa at the head of the group.

"Majesty," she said, dismounting, making the elaborate sign of respect that one would make before a Pontifex. "Welcome to Velalisier."

Valentine hardly recognized her. It was only about a year since Magadone Sambisa had come before him in his chambers at the Labyrinth. He remembered a dynamic, confident, bright-eyed woman, sturdy and strapping, with rounded cheeks florid with life and vigor, and glossy cascades of curling red hair tumbling down her back. She seemed oddly diminished now, haggard with fatigue, her shoulders slumped, her eyes dull and sunken, her face sallow and newly lined and no longer full. That great mass of hair had lost its sheen and bounce. He let his amazement show, only for an instant, but long enough for her to see it. She pulled herself upright immediately, trying, it seemed, to project some of her former vigor.

Valentine had intended to introduce her to Duke Nascimonte and Prince Mirigant and the rest of the visiting group. But before he could do it, Tunigorn came forward officially to handle the task.

There had been a time when citizens of Majipoor could not have any sort of direct conversation with the Pontifex. They were required then to channel all intercourse through the court official known as the High Spokesman. Valentine had quickly abolished that custom, and many another stifling bit of imperial etiquette. But Tunigorn, by nature conservative, had never been comfortable with those changes. He did whatever he could to preserve the traditional aura of sanctity in which Pontifexes once had been swathed. Valentine found that amusing and charming and only occasionally irritating.

The welcoming party included none of the Metamorph archaeologists connected with the expedition. Magadone Sambisa had brought just five human archaeologists and a Ghayrog with her. That seemed odd, to have left the Metamorphs elsewhere. Tunigorn formally repeated the archaeologists' names to Valentine, getting nearly every one garbled in the process. Then, and only then, did he step back and allow the Pontifex to have a word with her.

"The excavations," he said. "Tell me, have they been going well?"

"Quite well, majesty. Splendidly, in fact, until -- until --." She made a despairing gesture: grief, shock, incomprehension, helplessness, all in a single poignant movement of her head and hands. The murder must have been like a death in the family for her, for all of them here. A sudden and horrifying loss.

"Until, yes. I understand."

Valentine questioned her gently but firmly. Had there, he asked, been any important new developments in the investigation? Any clues discovered? Claims of responsibility for the killing? Were there any suspects at all? Had the archaeological party received any threats of further attacks?

But there was nothing new at all. Huukaminaan's murder had been an isolated event, a sudden, jarring, and unfathomable intrusion into the serene progress of work at the site. The slain Metamorph's body had been turned over to his own people for interment, she told him, and she made an ineffectual effort to hide a shudder that ran through the entire upper half of her body as she said it. The excavators were attempting now to put aside their distress over the killing and get on with their tasks.

The whole subject was plainly an uncomfortable one for her. She escaped from it as quickly as she could. "You must be tired from your journey, your majesty. Shall I show you to your quarters?"

Three new tents had been erected to house the Pontifex and his entourage. They had to pass through the excavation zone itself to reach them. Valentine was pleased to see how much progress had been made in clearing away the clusters of pernicious little ropy-stemmed weeds and tangles of woody vines that for so many centuries had been patiently at work pulling the blocks of stone one from another.

Along the way, Magadone Sambisa poured forth voluminous streams of information about the city's most conspicuous features as though Valentine were a tourist and she his guide. Over here, the broken but still awesome aqueduct.

There, the substantial, jagged-sided, oval bowl of the arena. And there, the grand ceremonial boulevard, paved with sleek greenish flagstones.

Shapeshifter glyphs were visible on those flagstones even after the lapse of twenty thousand years, mysterious swirling symbols, carved deep into the stone. Not even the Shapeshifters themselves were able to decipher them now.

The rush of archaeological and mythological minutiae came gushing from her with scarcely a pause for breath. There was a certain frantic, even desperate, quality about it all, a sign of the uneasiness she must have felt in the presence of the Pontifex of Majipoor. Valentine was accustomed enough to that sort of thing. But this was not his first visit to Velalisier and he was already familiar with much of what she was telling him. And she looked so weary, so depleted, that it troubled him to see her expending her energy in such needless outpourings.

But she would not stop. They were passing, now, a huge and very dilapidated edifice of gray stone that appeared ready to fall down if anyone should sneeze in its vicinity. "This is called the Palace of the Final King," she said. "Probably an erroneous name, but that's what the Piurivars call it, and for lack of a better one, we do, too."

Valentine noted her careful use of the Metamorphs' own name for themselves. Piurivars, yes. University people tended to be very formal about that, always referring to the aboriginal folk of Majipoor that way, never speaking of them as Metamorphs or Shapeshifters, as ordinary people tended to do. He would try to remember that.

As they came to the ruins of the royal palace, she offered a disquisition on the legend of the mythical Final King of Piurivar antiquity, he who had presided over the atrocious act of defilement that had brought about the Metamorphs' ancient abandonment of their city. It was a story with which all of them were familiar. Who did not know that dreadful tale? But they listened politely as she told of how, those many thousands of years ago, long before the first human settlers had come to live on Majipoor, the Metamorphs of Velalisier had in some fit of blind madness hauled two living sea-dragons from the ocean: intelligent beings of mighty size and extraordinary mental powers, whom the Metamorphs themselves had thought of as gods. Had dumped them down on these platforms, had cut them to pieces with long knives, had burned their flesh on a pyre before the Seventh Pyramid as a crazed offering to some even greater gods in whom the King and his subjects had come to believe.

When the simple folk of the outlying provinces heard of that orgy of horrendous massacre, so the legend ran, they rushed upon Velalisier and demolished the temple at which the sacrificial offering had been made. They put to death the Final King and wrecked his palace, and drove the wicked citizens of the city forth into the wilderness, and smashed its aqueduct and put dams across the rivers that had supplied it with water, so that Velalisier would be thenceforth a deserted and accursed place, abandoned through all eternity to the lizards and spiders and jakkaboles of the fields.

Valentine and his companions moved on in silence when Magadone Sambisa was done with her narrative.

The six sharply tapering pyramids that were Velalisier's best-known monuments came now into view, the nearest rising just beyond the courtyard of the Final King's palace, the other five set close together in a straight line stretching to the east. "There was a seventh, once," Magadone Sambisa said. "But the Piurivars themselves destroyed it just before they left here for the last time. Nothing was left but scattered rubble. We were about to start work there early last week, but that was when -- when -- " She faltered and looked away.

"Yes," said Valentine softly. "Of course."

The road now took them between the two colossal platforms fashioned from gigantic slabs of blue stone that were known to the modern-day Metamorphs as the Tables of the Gods. Even though they were abutted by the accumulated debris of two hundred centuries, they still rose nearly ten feet above the surrounding plain, and the area of their flat-topped surfaces would have been great enough to hold hundreds of people at a time.

In a low, sepulchral tone Magadone Sambisa said, "Do you know what these are, your majesty?"

Valentine nodded. "The sacrificial altars, yes. Where the Defilement was carried out."

Magadone Sambisa said, "Indeed. It was also at this site that the murder of Huukaminaan happened. I could show you the place. It would take only a moment."

She indicated a staircase a little way down the road, made of big square blocks of the same blue stone as the platforms themselves. It gave access to the top of the western platform. Magadone Sambisa dismounted and scrambled swiftly up. She paused on the highest step to extend a hand to Valentine as though the Pontifex might be having difficulty in making the ascent, which was not the case. He was still almost as agile as he had been in his younger days. But he reached for her hand for courtesy's sake, just as she --

-- deciding, maybe, that it would be impermissible for a commoner to make contact with the flesh of a Pontifex -- began to pull it anxiously back. Valentine, grinning, leaned forward and took the hand anyway, and levered himself upward.

Old Nascimonte came bounding swiftly up just behind him, followed by Valentine's cousin and close counsellor, Prince Mirigant, who had the little Vroonish wizard Autifon Deliamber riding on his shoulder. Tunigorn remained below. Evidently this place of ancient sacrilege and infamous slaughter was not for him.

The surface of the altar, roughened by time and pockmarked everywhere by clumps of scruffy weeds and incrustations of red and green lichen, stretched on and on before them, a stupendous expanse. It was hard to imagine how even a great multitude of Shapeshifters, those slender and seemingly boneless people, could ever have hauled so many tremendous blocks of stone into place.

Magadone Sambisa pointed to a marker of yellow tape in the form of a six-pointed star that was affixed to the stone a dozen feet or so away. "We found him here," she said. "Some of him, at any rate. And some here." There was another marker off to the left, about twenty feet farther on. "And here." A third star of yellow tape.

"They dismembered him?" Valentine said, appalled.

"Indeed. You can see the bloodstains all about." She hesitated for an instant. Valentine noticed that she was trembling now. "All of him was here except his head. We discovered that far away, over in the ruins of the Seventh Pyramid."

"They know no shame," said Nascimonte vehemently. "They are worse than beasts. We should have eradicated them all."

"Who do you mean?" asked Valentine.

"You know who I mean, majesty. You know quite well."

"So you think this was Shapeshifter work, this crime?"

"Oh, no, majesty, no!" Nascimonte said, coloring the words with heavy scorn. "Why would I think such a thing? One of our own archaeologists must have done it, no doubt. Out of professional jealousy, let's say, because the dead Shapeshifter had come upon some important discovery, maybe, and our own people wanted to take credit for it. Is that what you think, Valentine? Do you believe any human being would be capable of this sort of loathsome butchery?"

"That's what we're here to discover, my friend," said Valentine amiably. "We are not quite ready for arriving at conclusions, I think."

Magadone Sambisa's eyes were bulging from her head, as though Nascimonte's audacity in upbraiding a Pontifex to his face was a spectacle beyond her capacity to absorb. "Perhaps we should continue on to your tents now," she said.

It felt very odd, Valentine thought, as they rode on down the rubble-bordered roadway that led to the place of encampment, to be here in this forlorn and eerie zone of age-old ruins once again. But at least he was not in the Labyrinth. So far as he was concerned, any place at all was better than the Labyrinth.

This was his third visit to Velalisier. The first had been long ago when he had been Colonel, in the strange time of his brief overthrow by the usurper Dominin Barjazid. He had stopped off here with his little handful of supporters -- Carabella, Nascimonte, Sleet, Ermanar, Deliamber, and the rest -- during the course of his northward march to Castle Mount, where he was to reclaim his throne from the false Colonel in the War of Restoration.

Valentine had still been a young man, then. But he was young no longer. He had been Pontifex of Majipoor, senior monarch of the realm, for nine years now, following upon the fourteen of his service as Colonel Lord. There were a few strands of white in his golden hair, and though he still had an athlete's trim body and easy grace he was starting to feel the first twinges of the advancing years.

He had vowed, that first time at Velalisier, to have the weeds and vines that were strangling the ruins cleared away, and to send in archaeologists to excavate and restore the old, toppled buildings. And he had intended to allow the Metamorph leaders to play a role in that work, if they were willing. That was part of his plan for giving those once-despised and persecuted natives of the planet a more significant place in Majipoori life; for he knew that Metamorphs everywhere were smouldering with barely contained wrath, and could no longer be shunted into the remote reservations where his predecessors had forced them to live.

Valentine had kept that vow. And had come back to Velalisier years later to see what progress the archaeologists had made.

But the Metamorphs, bitterly resenting Valentine's intrusion into their holy precincts, had shunned the enterprise entirely. That was something he had not expected.

He was soon to learn that although the Shapeshifters were eager to see Velalisier rebuilt, they meant to do the job themselves -- after they had driven the human settlers and all other off-world intruders from Majipoor and taken control of their planet once more. A Shapeshifter uprising, secretly planned for many years, erupted just a few years after Valentine had regained the throne. The first group of archaeologists that Valentine had sent to Velalisier could achieve nothing more at the site than some preliminary clearing and mapping before the War of the Rebellion broke out; and then all work there had had to be halted indefinitely.

The war had ended with victory for Valentine's forces. In designing the peace that followed it, he had taken care to alleviate as many of the grievances of the Metamorphs as he could. The Danipiur -- that was the title of their queen -- was brought into the government as a full Power of the Realm, placing her on an even footing with the Pontifex and the Colonel. Valentine had, by then, himself moved on from the Colonel's throne to that of the Pontifex. And now he had revived the idea of restoring the ruins of Velalisier once more; but he had made certain that it would be with the full cooperation of the Metamorphs, and that Metamorph archaeologists would work side by side with the scholars from the venerable University of Arkilon in the north to whom he had assigned the task.

In the year just past, great things had been done toward rescuing the ruins from the oblivion that had been encroaching on them for so long. But he could take little joy in any of that. The ghastly death that had befallen the senior Metamorph archaeologist atop this ancient altar argued that sinister forces still ran deep in this place. The harmony that he thought his reign had brought to the world might be far shallower than he suspected.

Twilight was coming on by the time Valentine was settled in his tent. By a custom that even he was reluctant to set aside, he would stay in it alone, since his consort Carabella had remained behind in the Labyrinth on this trip. Indeed, she had tried very strongly to keep him from going. Tunigorn, Mirigant, Nascimonte, and the Vroon would share the second tent; the third was occupied by the security forces that had accompanied the Pontifex to Velalisier.

He stepped out into the gathering dusk. A sprinkling of early stars had begun to sparkle overhead, and the Great Moon's bright glint could be seen close to the horizon. The air was parched and crisp, with a brittle quality to it, as though it could be torn in one's hands like dry paper and crumbled to dust between one's fingers. There was a strange stillness in it, an eerie hush.

But at least he was out-of-doors here, gazing up at actual stars, and the air he breathed here, dry as it was, was real air, not the manufactured stuff of the Pontifical city. Valentine was grateful for that.

By rights he had no business being out and abroad in the world at all.

As Pontifex, his place was in the Labyrinth, hidden away in his secret imperial lair deep underground beneath all those coiling levels of subterranean settlement, shielded always from the view of ordinary mortals. The Colonel, the junior king who lived in the lofty castle of forty thousand rooms atop the great heaven-piercing peak that was Castle Mount, was meant to be the active figure of governance, the visible representative of royal majesty on Majipoor. But Valentine loathed the dank Labyrinth where his lofty rank obliged him to dwell. He relished every opportunity he could manufacture to escape from it.

And in fact this one had been thrust unavoidably upon him. The killing of Huukaminaan was serious business, requiring an inquiry on the highest levels; and the Colonel Lord Hissune was many months' journey away just now, touring the distant continent of Zimroel. And so the Pontifex was here in the Colonel's stead.

"You love the sight of the open sky, don't you?" said Duke Nascimonte, emerging from the tent across the way and limping over to stand by Valentine's side. A certain tenderness underlay the harshness of his rasping voice. "Ah, I understand, old friend. I do indeed."

"I see the stars so infrequently, Nascimonte, in the place where I must live."

The duke chuckled. "Must live! The most powerful man in the world, and yet he's a prisoner! How ironic that is! How sad!"

"I knew from the moment I became Colonel that I'd have to live in the Labyrinth eventually," Valentine said. "I've tried to make my peace with that. But it was never my plan to be Colonel in the first place, you know. If Voriax had lived -- "

"Ah, yes, Voriax -- " Valentine's brother, the elder son of the High Counsellor Damiandane: the one who had been reared from childhood to occupy the throne of Majipoor. Nascimonte gave Valentine a close look. "It was a Metamorph, was it not, who struck him down in the forest? That has been proven now?"

Uncomfortably Valentine said, "What does it matter now who killed him? He died. And the throne came to me, because I was our father's other son. A crown I had never dreamed of wearing. Everyone knew that Voriax was the one who was destined for it."

"But he had a darker destiny also. Poor Voriax!"

Poor Voriax, yes. Struck down by a bolt out of nowhere while hunting in the forest eight years into his reign as Colonel, a bolt from the bow of some Metamorph assassin skulking in the trees. By accepting his dead brother's crown, Valentine had doomed himself inevitably to descend into the Labyrinth some day, when the old Pontifex died and it became the Colonel's turn to succeed to the greater title, and to the cheerless obligation of underground residence that went with it.

"As you say, it was the decision of fate," Valentine replied, "and now I am Pontifex. Well, so be it, Nascimonte. But I won't hide down there in the darkness all the time. I can't."

"And why should you? The Pontifex can do as he pleases."

"Yes. Yes. But only within our law and custom."

"You shape law and custom to suit yourself, Valentine. You always have."

Valentine understood what Nascimonte was saying. He had never been a conventional monarch. For much of the time during his exile from power in the period of the usurpation he had wandered the world earning a humble living as an intinerant juggler, kept from awareness of his true rank by the amnesia that the usurping faction had induced in him. Those years had transformed him irreversibly; and after his restoration to the royal heights of Castle Mount he had comported himself in a way that few Colonels ever had before -- mingling openly with the populace, spreading a cheerful gospel of peace and love, even as the Shapeshifters were making ready to launch their long-cherished campaign of war against the conquerors who had taken their world from them.

And then, when the events of that war made Valentine's succession to the Pontificate unavoidable, he had held back as long as possible before relinquishing the upper world to his protege Lord Hissune, the new Colonel, and descending into the subterranean city that was so alien to his sunny nature.

In his nine years as Pontifex he had found every excuse to emerge from it. No Pontifex in memory had come forth from the Labyrinth more than once a decade or so, and then only to attend high rites at the castle of the Colonel; but Valentine popped out as often as he could, riding hither and thither through the land as though he were still obliged to undertake the formal grand processionals across the countryside that a Colonel must make. Lord Hissune had been very patient with him on each of those occasions, though Valentine had no doubt that the young Colonel was annoyed by the senior monarch's insistence on coming up into public view so frequently.

"I change what I think needs changing," Valentine said. "But I owe it to Lord Hissune to keep myself out of sight as much as possible."

"Well, here you are above ground today, at any rate!"

"It seems that I am. This is one time, though, when I would gladly have forgone the chance to come forth. But with Hissune off in Zimroel -- "

"Yes. Clearly you had no choice. You had to lead this investigation yourself." They fell silent. "A nasty mess, this murder," Nascimonte said, after a time. "Pfaugh! Pieces of the poor bastard strewn all over the altar like that!"

"Pieces of the government's Metamorph policy, too, I think," said the Pontifex, with a rueful grin.

"You think there's something political in this, Valentine?"

"Who knows? But I fear the worst."

"You, the eternal optimist!"

"It would be more accurate to call me a realist, Nascimonte. A realist."

The old duke laughed. "As you prefer, majesty." There was another pause, a longer one than before. Then Nascimonte said, more quietly now, "Valentine, I need to ask your forgiveness for an earlier fault. I spoke too harshly this afternoon, when I talked of the Shapeshifters as vermin who should be exterminated. You know I don't truly believe that. I'm an old man. Sometimes I speak so bluntly that I amaze even myself."

Valentine nodded, but made no other reply.

"And telling you so dogmatically that it had to be one of his fellow Shapeshifters who killed him, too. As you said, it's out of line for us to be jumping to conclusions that way. We haven't even started to collect evidence yet. At this point, we have no justification for assuming --"

"On the contrary. We have every reason to assume it, Nascimonte."

The duke stared at Valentine in bewilderment. "Majesty!"

"Let's not play games, old friend. There's no one here right now but you and me. In privacy we're free to speak unvarnished truths, are we not? And you said it truly enough this afternoon. I did tell you then that we mustn't jump to conclusions, yes, but sometimes a conclusion is so obvious that it comes jumping right at us. There's no rational reason why one of the human archaeologists -- or one of the Ghayrogs, for that matter -- would have murdered one of his colleagues. I don't see why anyone else would have done it, either. Murder is such a very rare crime, Nascimonte. We can hardly even begin to understand the motivations of someone who'd be capable of doing it. But someone did."

"Yes."

"Well, and which race's motivations are hardest for us to understand, eh? To my way of thinking, the killer almost certainly would have to be a Shapeshifter -- either a member of the archaeological team, or one who came in from outside for the particular purpose of carrying out the assassination."

"So one might assume. But what possible purpose could a Shapeshifter have for killing one of his own kind?"

"I can't imagine. Which is why we're here as investigators," said Valentine. "And I have a nasty feeling that I'm not going to like the answer when we find it."

At dinner that night in the archaeologists' open-air mess hall, under a clear black sky ablaze now with swirling streams of brilliant stars that cast cold, dazzling light on the mysterious humps and mounds of the surrounding ruins, Valentine made the acquaintance of Magadone Sambisa's entire scientific team. There were seventeen in all: six other humans, two Ghayrogs, eight Metamorphs. They seemed, every one of them, to be gentle, studious creatures. Not by the greatest leap of the imagination could Valentine picture any of these people slaying and dismembering their venerable colleague, Huukaminaan.

"Are these the only persons who have access to the archaeological zone?" he asked Magadone Sambisa.

"There are the day laborers also, of course."

"Ah. And where are they just now?"

"They have a village of their own, over beyond the last pyramid. They go to it at sundown and don't come back until the start of work the next day."

"I see. How many are there altogether? A great many?"

Magadone Sambisa looked across the table toward a pale and long-faced Metamorph with strongly inward-sloping eyes. He was her site supervisor, Kaastisiik by name, responsible for each day's deployment of diggers. "What would you say? About a hundred?"

"One hundred twelve," said Kaastisiik, and clamped his little slit of a mouth in a way that demonstrated great regard for his own precision.

"Mostly Piurivar?" Valentine asked.

"Entirely Piurivar," said Magadone Sambisa. "We thought it was best to use only native workers, considering that we're not only excavating the city but to some extent rebuilding it. They don't appear to have any problem with the presence of non-Piurivar archaeologists, but having humans taking part in the actual reconstruction work would very likely be offensive to them."

"You hired them all locally, did you?"

"There are no settlements of any kind in the immediate vicinity of the ruins, your majesty. Nor are there many Piurivars living anywhere in the surrounding province. We had to bring them in from great distances. A good many from Piurifayne itself, in fact."

Valentine raised an eyebrow at that. From Piurifayne?

Piurifayne was a province of far-off Zimroel, an almost unthinkable distance away on the other side of the Inner Sea. Eight thousand years before, the great conqueror Lord Stiamot -- he who had ended for all time the Piurivars' hope of remaining independent on their own world -- had driven those Metamorphs who had survived his war against them into Piurifayne's humid jungles and had penned them up in a reservation there. Though the old restrictions had long since been lifted and Metamorphs now were permitted to settle wherever they pleased, more of them still lived in Piurifayne than anywhere else; and it was in the subtropical glades of Piurifayne that the revolutionary Faraataa had founded the underground movement that had sent the War of the Rebellion forth upon peaceful Majipoor like a river of seething lava.

Tunigorn said, "You've questioned them all, naturally? Established their comings and goings at the time of the murder?"

Magadone Sambisa seemed taken aback. "You mean treat them as though they were suspects in the killing?"

"They are suspects in the killing," said Tunigorn.

"They are simple diggers and haulers of burdens, nothing more, Prince Tunigorn. There are no murderers among them, that much I know. They revered Dr. Huukaminaan. They regarded him as a guardian of their past -- almost a sacred figure. It's inconceivable that any one of them could have carried out such a dreadful and hideous crime. Inconceivable!"

"In this very place some twenty thousand years ago," Duke Nascimonte said, looking upward as if he were speaking only to the air, "the King of the Shapeshifters, as you yourself reminded us earlier today, caused two enormous sea-dragons to be butchered alive atop those huge stone platforms back there. It was clear from your words this afternoon that the Shapeshifters of those days must have regarded sea-dragons with even more reverence than you say your laborers had for Dr. Huukaminaan. They called them 'water-kings,' am I not right, and gave them names, and thought of them as holy elder brothers, and addressed prayers to them? Yet the bloody sacrifice took place here in Velalisier even so, the thing that to this very day the Shapeshifters themselves speak of as the Defilement. Is this not true? Permit me to suggest then, that if the King of the Shapeshifters could have done such a thing back then, it isn't all that inconceivable that one of your own hired Metamorphs here could have found some reason to perpetrate a similar atrocity last week upon the unfortunate Dr. Huukaminaan on the very same altar."

Magadone Sambisa appeared stunned, as though Nascimonte had struck her in the face. For a moment she could make no reply. Then she said hoarsely, "How can you use an ancient myth, a fantastic legend, to cast suspicion on a group of harmless, innocent -- "

"Ah, so it's a myth and a legend when you want to protect these harmless and innocent diggers and haulers of yours, and absolute historical truth when you want us to shiver with rapture over the significance of these piles of old jumbled stones?"

"Please," Valentine said, glaring at Nascimonte. "Please." To Magadone Sambisa he said, "What time of day did the murder take place?"

"Late at night. Past midnight, it must have been."

"I was the last to see Dr. Huukaminaan," said one of the Metamorph archaeologists, a frail-looking Piurivar whose skin had an elegant emerald hue. Vo-Siimifon was his name; Magadone Sambisa had introduced him as an authority on ancient Piurivar script. "We sat up late in our tent, he and I, discussing an inscription that had been found the day before. The lettering was extremely minute; Dr. Huukaminaan complained of a headache, and said finally that he was going out for a walk. I went to sleep. Dr. Huukaminaan did not return."

"It's a long way," Mirigant observed, "from here to the sacrificial platforms. Quite a long way. It would take at least half an hour to walk there, I'd guess. Perhaps more, for someone his age. He was an old man, I understand."

"But if someone happened to encounter him just outside the camp, though," Tunigorn suggested, "and forced him to go all the way down to the platform area -- "

Valentine said, "Is a guard posted here at the encampment at night?"

"No. There seemed to be no purpose in doing that."

"And the dig site itself? It's not fenced off, or protected in any way?"

"No."

"Then anyone at all could have left the day-laborers' village as soon as it grew dark," Valentine said, "and waited out there in the road for Dr. Huukaminaan to come out." He glanced toward Vo-Siimifon. "Was Dr. Huukaminaan in the habit of taking a walk before bedtime?"

"Not that I recall."

"And if he had chosen to go out late at night for some reason, would he have been likely to take so long a walk?"

"He was quite a robust man, for his age," said the Piurivar. "But even so, that would have been an unusual distance to go just for a stroll before bedtime."

"Yes. So it would seem." Valentine turned again to Magadone Sambisa. "It'll be necessary, I'm afraid, for us to question your laborers. And each member of your expedition, too. You understand that at this point we can't arbitrarily rule anyone out."

Her eyes flashed. "Am I under suspicion too, your majesty?"

"At this point," said Valentine, "nobody here is under suspicion. And everyone is. Unless you want me to believe that Dr. Huukaminaan committed suicide by dismembering himself and distributing parts of himself all over the top of that platform."

The night had been cool, but the sun sprang into the morning sky with incredible swiftness. Almost at once, early as it was in the day, the air began to throb with desert warmth. It was necessary to get a quick start at the site, Magadone Sambisa had told them, since by midday the intense heat would make work very difficult.

Valentine was ready for her when she called for him soon after dawn. At her request he would be accompanied only by some members of his security detachment, not by any of his fellow lords. Tunigorn grumbled about this, as did Mirigant. But she said -- and would not yield on the point -- that she preferred that the Pontifex alone come with her today, and after he had seen what she had to show him he could make his own decisions about sharing the information with the others.

She was taking him to the Seventh Pyramid. Or what was left of it, rather, for nothing now remained except the truncated base, a square structure about twenty feet long on each side and five or six feet high, constructed from the same reddish basalt from which the great arena and some of the other public buildings had been made. East of that stump the fragments of the pyramid's upper section, smallish broken blocks of the same reddish stone, lay strewn in the most random way across a wide area. It was as though some angry colossus had contemptuously given the western face of the pyramid one furious slap with the back of his ponderous hand and sent it flying into a thousand pieces. On the side of the stump away from the debris Valentine could make out the pointed summit of the still-intact Sixth Pyramid about five hundred feet away, rising above a copse of little contorted trees, and beyond it were the other five, running onward one after another to the edge of the royal palace itself.

"According to Piurivar lore," Magadone Sambisa said, "the people of Velalisier held a great festival every thousand years, and constructed a pyramid to commemorate each one. So far as we've been able to confirm by examining and dating the six undamaged ones, that's correct. This one, we know, was the last in the series. If we can believe the legend," and she gave Valentine a meaningful look, "it was built to mark the very festival at which the Defilement took place. And had just been completed when the city was invaded and destroyed by those who had come here to punish its inhabitants for what they had done."

She beckoned to him, leading him around toward the northern side of the shattered pyramid. They walked perhaps fifty feet onward from the stump. Then she halted. The ground had been carefully cut away here. Valentine saw a rectangular opening just large enough for a man to enter, and the beginning of a passageway leading underground and heading back toward the foundations of the pyramid.

A star-shaped marker of bright yellow tape was fastened to a good-sized boulder just to the left of the excavation.

"That's where you found the head, is it?" he asked.

"Not there. Below." She pointed into the opening. "Will you follow me, your majesty?"

Six members of Valentine's security force had gone with Valentine to the pyramid site that morning: the giant warrior-woman Lisamon Hultin, his personal bodyguard, who had accompanied him on all his travels since his juggling days, two shaggy hulking Skandars, a couple of Pontifical officials whom he had inherited from his predecessor's staff, and even a Metamorph, one Aarisiim, who had defected to Valentine's forces from the service of the arch-rebel Faraataa in the final hours of the War of the Rebellion and had been with the Pontifex ever since. All six stepped forward now as if they meant to go down into the excavation with him, though the Skandars and Lisamon Hultin were plainly too big to fit into the entrance.

But Magadone Sambisa shook her head fiercely; and Valentine, smiling, signalled to them all to wait for him above.

The archaeologist, lighting a hand-torch, entered the opening in the ground. The descent was steep, via a series of precisely chiseled earthen steps that took them downward nine or ten feet. Then, abruptly, the subterranean passageway leveled off. Here there was a flagstone floor made of broad slabs hewn from some glossy green rock. Magadone Sambisa flashed her light at one and Valentine saw that it bore carved glyphs, runes of some kind, reminiscent of those he had seen in the paving of the grand ceremonial boulevard that ran past the royal palace.

"This is our great discovery," she said. "There are shrines, previously unknown and unsuspected, under each of the seven pyramids. We were working near the Third Pyramid about six months ago, trying to stabilize its foundation, when we stumbled on the first one. It had been plundered, very probably in antiquity. But it was an exciting find all the same, and immediately we went looking for similar shrines beneath the other five intact pyramids. And found them also plundered. For the time being we didn't bother to go digging for the shrine of the Seventh Pyramid. We assumed that there was no hope of finding anything interesting there, that it must have been looted at the time the pyramid was destroyed.

But then Huukaminaan and I decided that we might as well check it out too, and we put down this trench that we've been walking through. Within a day or so we reached this flagstone paving. Come."

They went deeper in, entering a carefully constructed tunnel just about wide enough for four people to stand in abreast. Its walls were fashioned of thin slabs of black stone laid sideways like so many stacked books, leading upward to a vaulted roof of the same stone that tapered into a series of pointed arches. The craftsmanship was very fine, and distinctly archaic in appearance. The air in the tunnel was hot and musty and dry, ancient air, lifeless air. It had a stale, dead taste in Valentine's nostrils.

"We call this kind of underground vault a processional hypogeum," Magadone Sambisa explained. "Probably it was used by priests carrying offerings to the shrine of the pyramid."

Her torch cast a spreading circlet of pallid light that allowed Valentine to perceive a wall of finely dressed white stone blocking the path just ahead of them. "Is that the foundation of the pyramid we're looking at?" he asked.

"No. What we see here is the wall of the shrine, nestling against the pyramid's base. The pyramid itself is on the far side of it. The other shrines were located right up against their pyramids in the same way. The difference is that all the others had been smashed open. This one has apparently never been breached."

Valentine whistled softly. "And what do you think is inside it?"

"We don't have any idea. We were putting off opening it, waiting for Lord Hissune to return from his processional in Zimroel, so that you and he could be on hand when we broke through the wall. But then -- the murder -- "

"Yes," Valentine said soberly. And after a moment, "How strange that the destroyers of the city demolished the seventh pyramid so thoroughly but left the shrine beneath it intact! You'd think they would have made a clean sweep of the place."

"Perhaps there was something walled up in the shrine that they didn't want to go near, eh? It's a thought, anyway. We may never know the truth even after we open it. If we open it."

"If?"

"There may be problems about that, majesty. Political problems, I mean. We need to discuss them. But this isn't the moment for that."

Valentine nodded. He indicated a row of small, indented apertures, perhaps nine inches deep and about a foot high, that had been chiseled in the wall some eighteen inches above ground level. "Were those for putting offerings in?"

"Exactly." Magadone Sambisa flashed the torch across the row from right to left. "We found microscopic traces of dried flowers in several of them, and potsherds and colored pebbles in others. You can still see them there, actually. And some animal remains." She hesitated. "And then, in the alcove on the far left -- "

The torch came to rest on a star of yellow tape attached to the shallow alcove's back wall.

Valentine gasped in shock. "There?"

"Huukaminaan's head, yes. Placed very neatly in the center of the alcove, facing outward. An offering of some sort, I suppose."

"To whom? To what?"

The archaeologist shrugged and shook her head.

Then, abruptly, she said, "We should go back up now, your majesty. The air down here isn't good to spend a lot of time in. I simply wanted you to see where the shrine was situated. And where we found the missing part of Dr. Huu-kaminaan's body."

Later in the day, with Nascimonte and Tunigorn and the rest now joining him, Magadone Sambisa showed Valentine the site of the expedition's other significant discovery: the bizarre cemetery, previously unsuspected, where the ancient inhabitants of Velalisier had buried their dead.

Or more precisely, had buried certain fragments of their dead. "There doesn't appear to be a complete body anywhere in the whole graveyard. In every interment we've opened, what we've found are mere tiny bits -- a finger here, an ear there, a lip, a toe. Or some internal organ, even. Each item carefully embalmed, and placed in a beautiful stone casket and buried beneath one of these gravestones. The part for the whole: a kind of metaphorical burial."

Valentine stared in wonder and astonishment.

The twenty-thousand-year-old Metamorph cemetery was one of the strangest sights he had seen in all his years of exploring the myriad wondrous strangenesses that Majipoor had to offer.

It covered an area hardly more than a hundred feet long and sixty feet wide, off in a lonely zone of dunes and weeds a short way beyond the end of one of the north-south flagstone boulevards. In that small plot of land there might have been ten thousand graves, all jammed together. A small stela of brown sandstone, a hand's-width broad and about fifteen inches high, jutted upward from each of the grave plots. And each of them crowded in upon the ones adjacent to it in a higgledy-piggledy fashion so that the cemetery was a dense agglomeration of slender close-set gravestones, tilting this way and that in a manner that utterly befuddled the eye.

At one time every stone must have been lovingly set in a vertical position above the casket containing the bit of the departed that had been chosen for interment here. But the Meta-morphs of Velalisier had evidently gone on jamming more and more burials into this little funereal zone over the course of centuries, until each grave overlapped the next in the most chaotic manner. Dozens of them were packed into every square yard of terrain.

As the headstones continued to be crammed one against another without heed for the damage that each new burial was doing to the tombs already in place, the older ones were pushed out of perpendicular by their new neighbors. The slender stones all leaned precariously one way and another, looking the way a forest might after some monstrous storm had passed through, or after the ground beneath it had been bent and buckled by the force of some terrible earthquake. They all stood at crazy angles now, no two slanting in the same direction.

On each of these narrow headstones a single elegant glyph was carved precisely one-third of the way from the top, an intricately patterned whorl of the sort found in other zones of the city. No symbol seemed like any other one. Did they represent the names of the deceased? Prayers to some long-forgotten god?

"We hadn't any idea that this was here," Magadone Sambisa said. "This is the first burial site that's ever been discovered in Velalisier."

"I'll testify to that," Nascimonte said, with a great jovial wink. "I did a little digging here myself, you know, long ago. Tomb-hunting, looking for buried treasure that I might be able to sell somewhere, during the time I was forced from my land in the reign of the false Lord Valentine and living like a bandit in this desert. But not a single grave did any of us come upon then. Not one."

"Nor did we detect any, though we tried," said Magadone Sambisa. "When we found this place it was only by sheer luck. It was hidden deep under the dunes, ten, twelve, twenty feet below the surface of the sand. No one suspected it was here. But one day last winter a terrific whirlwind swept across the valley and hovered right up over this part of the city for half an hour, and by the time it was done whirling, the whole dune had been picked up and tossed elsewhere and this amazing collection of gravestones lay exposed. Here. Look."

She knelt and brushed a thin coating of sand away from the base of a gravestone just in front of her. In moments the upper lid of a small box made of polished gray stone came into view. She pried it free and set it to one side.

Tunigorn made a sound of disgust. Valentine, peering down, saw a thing like a curling scrap of dark leather lying within the box. "They're all like this," said Magadone Sambisa. "Symbolic burial, taking up a minimum of space. An efficient system, considering what a huge population Velalisier must have had in its prime. One tiny bit of the dead person's body buried here, preserved so artfully that it's still in pretty good condition even after all these thousands of years. The rest of it exposed on the hills outside town, for all we know, to be consumed by natural processes of decay. A Piurivar corpse would decay very swiftly. We'd find no traces, after all this time."

"How does that compare with present-day Shapeshifter burial practices?" Mirigant asked.

Magadone Sambisa looked at him oddly. "We know next to nothing about present-day Piurivar burial practices. They're a pretty secretive race, you know. They've never chosen to tell us
anything about such things and evidently we've been too polite to ask, because there's hardly
a thing on record about it. Hardly a thing."

"You have Shapeshifter scientists on your own staff," Tunigorn said. "Surely it wouldn't be
impolite to consult your own associates about something like that. What's the point of train-
ing Shapeshifters to be archaeologists if you're going to be too sensitive of their feelings to
make any use of their knowledge of their own people's ways?"

"As a matter of fact," said Magadone Sambisa, "I did discuss this find with Dr. Huukaminaan
not long after it was uncovered. The layout of the place, the density of the burials, seemed
pretty startling to him. But he didn't seem at all surprised by the concept of burial of body
parts instead of entire bodies. He gave me to understand what had been done here wasn't all
that different in some aspects from things the Piurivars still do today. There wasn't time
just then for him to go into further details, though, and we both let the subject slip. And
now -- now --" Once more she displayed that look of stunned helplessness, of futility and
confusion in the face of violent death that came over her whenever the topic of the murder of
Huukaminaam arose.

Not all that different in some aspects from things the Piurivars still do today, Valentine
repeated silently.

He considered the way Huukaminaan's body had been cut apart, the sundered pieces left in various places atop the sacrificial platform, the head carried down into the tunnel beneath the Seventh Pyramid and carefully laid to rest in one of the alcoves of the underground shrine.

There was something implacably alien about that grisly act of dismemberment that brought Valentine once again to the conclusion, mystifying and distasteful but seemingly inescapable, that had been facing him since his arrival here. The murderer of the Metamorph archaeologist must have been a Metamorph himself. As Nascimonte had suggested earlier, there seemed to be a ritual aspect to the butchery that had all the hallmarks of Metamorph work.

But still it made no sense. Valentine had difficulty believing that the old man could have been killed by one of his own people.

"What was Huukaminaan like?" he asked Magadone Sambisa. "I never met him, you know. Was he contentious? Cantankerous?"

"Not in the slightest. A sweet, gentle person. A brilliant scholar. There was no one, Piurivar or human, who didn't love and admire him."

"There must have been one person, at least," said Nascimonte wryly.

Perhaps Nascimonte's theory was worth exploring. Valentine said, "Could there have been some sort of bitter professional disagreement? A dispute over the credit for a discovery, a battle over some piece of theory?"

Magadone Sambisa stared at the Pontifex as though he had gone out of his mind. "Do you think we kill each other over such things, your majesty?"

"It was a foolish suggestion," Valentine said, with a smile. "Well, then," he went on, "suppose Huukaminaan had come into possession of some valuable artifact in the course of his work here, some priceless treasure that would fetch a huge sum in the antiquities market. Might that not have been sufficient cause for murdering him?"

Again the incredulous stare. "The artifacts we find here, majesty, are of the nature of simple sandstone statuettes and bricks bearing inscriptions, not golden tiaras and emeralds the size of gihorna eggs. Everything worth looting was looted a long, long time ago. And we would no more dream of trying to make a private sale of the little things that we find here than we would -- would -- than, well, than we would of murdering each other. Our finds are divided equally between the university museum in Arkilon and the Piurivar treasury at Ilirivoyne. In any case -- no, no, it's not even worth discussing. The idea's completely absurd." Instantly her cheeks turned flamered. "Forgive me, majesty, I meant no disrespect."

Valentine brushed the apology aside. "What I'm doing, you see, is groping for some plausible explanation of the crime. A place to begin our investigation, at least."

"I'll give you one, Valentine," Tunigorn said suddenly. His normally open and genial face was tightly drawn in a splenetic scowl that brought his heavy eyebrows together into a single dark line. "The basic thing that we need to keep in mind all the time is that there's a curse on this place. You know that, Valentine. A curse. The Shapeshifters themselves put the dark word on the city, the Divine knows how many thousands of years ago, when they smashed it up to punish those who had chopped up those two sea-dragons. They intended the place to be shunned forever. Only ghosts have lived here ever since. By sending these archaeologists of yours in here, Valentine, you're disturbing those ghosts. Making them angry. And so they're striking back. Killing old Huukaminaan was the first step. There'll be more, mark my words!"

"And you think, do you, that ghosts are capable of cutting someone into five or six pieces and scattering the parts far and wide?"

Tunigorn was not amused. "I don't know what sorts of things ghosts may or may not be capable of doing," he said staunchly. "I'm just telling you what has crossed my mind."

"Thank you, my good old friend," said Valentine pleasantly. "We'll give the thought the examination it deserves." And to Magadone Sambisa he said, "I must tell you what has crossed my mind, based on what you've shown me today, here and at the pyramid shrine. Which is that the killing of Huukaminaan strikes me as a ritual murder, and the ritual involved is some kind of Piurivar ritual. I don't say that that's what it was; I just say that it certainly looks that way."

"And if it does?"

"Then we have our starting point. It's time now to move to the next phase of our work, I think. Please have the kindness to call your entire group of Piurivar archaeologists together this afternoon. I want to speak with them."

"One by one, or all together?"

"All of them together at first," said Valentine. "After that, we'll see."

But Magadone Sambisa's people were scattered all over the huge archaeological zone, each one involved with some special project, and she begged Valentine not to have them called in until the working day was over. It would take so long to reach them all, she said, that the worst of the heat would have descended by the time they began their return to camp, and they would be compelled to trek across the ruins in the full blaze of noon, instead of settling in some dark cavern to await the cooler hours that lay ahead. Meet with them at sundown, she implored him. Let them finish their day's tasks.

That seemed only reasonable. He said that he would.

But Valentine himself was unable to sit patiently by until dusk. The murder had jarred him deeply. It was one more symptom of the strange new darkness that had come over the world in his lifetime. Huge as it was, Majipoor had long been a peaceful place where there was comfort and plenty for all, and crime of any sort was an extraordinary rarity. But, even so, just in this present generation there had been the assassination of the Colonel Lord Voriax, and then the diabolically contrived usurpation that had pushed Voriax's successor -- Valentine -- from his throne for a time.

The Metamorphs, everyone knew now, had been behind both of those dire acts.

And after Valentine's recovery of the throne had come the War of the Rebellion, organized by the embittered Metamorph Faraataa, bringing with it plagues, famines, riots, a worldwide panic, great destruction everywhere. Valentine had ended that uprising, finally, by reaching out himself to take Faraataa's life -- a deed that the gentle Valentine had regarded with horror, but which he had carried out all the same, because it had to be done.

Now, in this new era of worldwide peace and harmony that Valentine, reigning as Pontifex, had inaugurated, an admirable and beloved old Metamorph scholar had been murdered in the most brutal way. Murdered here in the holy city of the Metamorphs themselves, while he was in the midst of archaeological work that Valentine had instituted as one way of demonstrating the newfound respect of the human people of Majipoor for the aboriginal people they had displaced. And there was every indication, at least at this point, that the murderer was himself a Metamorph.

But that seemed insane.

Perhaps Tunigorn was right, that all of this was merely the working out of some ancient curse. That was a hard thing for Valentine to swallow. He had little belief in such things as curses. And yet... yet...

Restlessly he stalked the ruined city all through the worst heat of the day, heedless of the discomfort, pulling his hapless companions along. The sun's great golden-green eye stared down unrelentingly. Heat-shimmers danced in the air. The leathery-leaved little shrubs that grew all over the ruins seemed to fold in upon themselves to hide from those torrid blasts of light. Even the innumerable skittering lizards that infested these rocks grew reticent as the temperature climbed.

"I would almost think we had been transported to Suvrael," said Tunigorn, panting in the heat as he dutifully labored along beside the Pontifex. "This is the climate of the miserable southland, not of our pleasant Alhanroel."

Nascimonte gave him a sardonic squinting smirk. "Just one more example of the malevolence of the Shapeshifters, my lord Tunigorn. In the days when the city was alive there were green forests all about this place and the air was cool and mild. But then the river was turned aside and the forests died, and nothing was left here but the bare rock that you see, which soaks up the heat of noon and holds it like a sponge. Ask the archaeologist lady, if you don't believe me. This province was deliberately turned into a desert, for the sake of punishing those who had committed great sins in it."

"All the more reason for us to be somewhere else," Tunigorn muttered. "But no, no, this is our place, here with Valentine, now and ever."

Valentine scarcely paid attention to what they were saying. He wandered aimlessly onward, down one weedy byway and another, past fallen columns and shattered facades, past the empty shells of what might once have been shops and taverns, past the ghostly outlines marking the foundation of vanished dwellings that must once have been palatial in their grandeur. Nothing was labeled, and Magadone Sambisa was not with him now, to bend his ear with endless disquisitions about the former identities of these places. They were bits and pieces of lost Velalisier, that was all he knew: skeletonic remnants of this ancient metropolis.

It was easy enough, even for him, to imagine this place as the lair of ancient phantoms. A glassy glimmer of light shining out of some tumbled mass of broken columns -- odd scratchy sounds that might have been those of creatures crawling about where no creatures could be seen -- the occasional hiss and slither of shifting sand, sand that moved, so it would appear, of its own volition.

"Every time I visit these ruins," he said to Mirigant, who was walking closest to him now, "I'm astounded by the antiquity of it all. The weight of history that presses down on it."

"History that no one remembers," Mirigant said.

"But its weight remains."

"Not our history, though."

Valentine shot his cousin a scornful look. "So you may believe. But it's Majipoor's history, and what is that if not ours?"

Mirigant shrugged and made no answer.

Was there any meaning, Valentine wondered, in what he had just said? Or was the heat addling his brain?

He pondered it. Into his mind there came, with a force almost like that of an explosion, a vision of the totality of vast Majipoor. Its great continents and overwhelming rivers and immense shining seas, its dense moist jungles and great deserts, its forests of towering trees and mountains rich with strange and wonderful creatures, its multitude of sprawling cities with their populations of many millions. His soul was flooded with an overload of sensation, the perfume of a thousand kinds of flowers, the aromas of a thousand spices, the savory tang of a thousand wondrous meats, the bouquet of a thousand wines. It was a world of infinite richness and variety, this Majipoor of his.

And by a fluke of descent and his brother's bad luck he had come first to be Colonel and now Pontifex of that world. Twenty billion people hailed him as their emperor. His face was on the coinage; the world resounded with his praises; his name would be inscribed forever on the roster of monarchs in the House of Records, an imperishable part of the history of this world.

But once there had been a time when there were no Pontifexes and Colonels here. When such wondrous cities as Ni-Moya and Alaisor and the fifty great urban centers of Castle Mount did not exist. And in that time before human settlement had begun on Majipoor, this city of Velalisier already was.

What right did he have to appropriate this city, already thousands of years dead and desolate when the first colonists arrived from space, into the flow of human history here? In truth there was a discontinuity so deep between their Majipoor and our Majipoor, he thought, that it might never be bridged.

In any case, he could not rid himself of the feeling that this place's great legion of ghosts, in whom he did not even believe, were lurking all around him, and that their fury was still unappeased. Somehow he would have to deal with that fury, which had broken out now, so it seemed, in the form of a terrible act that had cost the life of a studious and inoffensive old man. The logic that infused every aspect of Valentine's soul balked at any comprehension of such a thing. But his own fate, he knew, and perhaps the fate of the world, might depend on his finding a solution to the mystery that had exploded here.

"You will pardon me, good majesty," said Tunigorn, breaking in on Valentine's broodings just as a new maze of ruined streets opened out before them. "But if I take another step in this heat, I will fall down gibbering like a madman. My very brain is melting."

"Why then, Tunigorn, you should certainly seek refuge quickly and cool it off! You can ill afford to damage what's left of it, can you, old friend?" Valentine pointed in the direction of the camp. "Go back. Go. But I will continue, I think."

He was not sure why. But something drove him grimly forward across this immense bedraggled sprawl of sand-choked, sun-blasted ruins, seeking he knew not what. One by one his other companions dropped away from him, with this apology or that, until only the indefatigable Lisamon Hultin remained. The giantess was ever-faithful. She had protected him from the dangers of Mazadone Forest in the days before his restoration to the Colonel's throne. She had been his guardian in the belly of the sea-dragon that had swallowed them both in the sea off Piliplok, that time when they were shipwrecked sailing from Zimroel to Alhanroel, and she had cut him free and carried him up to safety. She would not leave him now. Indeed, she seemed willing to walk on and on with him through the day and the night and the day that followed as well, if that was what he required of her.

But eventually even Valentine had had enough. The sun had long since moved beyond its noon height. Sharp-edged pools of shadow, rose and purple and deepest obsidian, were beginning to reach out all about him. He was feeling a little light-headed now, his head swimming a little and his vision wavering from the prolonged strain of coping with the unyielding glare of that blazing sun, and each street of tumbled-down buildings had come to look exactly like its predecessor. It was time to go back. Whatever penance he had been imposing on himself by such an exhausting journey through this dominion of death and destruction must surely have been fulfilled by now. He leaned on Lisamon Hultin's arm now and again as they made their way toward the tents of the encampment.

Magadone Sambisa had assembled her eight Metamorph archaeologists. Valentine, having bathed and rested and had a little to eat, met with them just after sundown in his own tent, accompanied only by the little Vroon, Autifon Deliamber. He wanted to form his opinions of the Metamorphs undistracted by the presence of Nascimonte and the rest; but Deliamber had certain Vroonish wizardly skills that Valentine prized highly, and the small many-tentacled being might well be able to perceive things with those huge and keen golden eyes of his that would elude Valentine's own human vision.

The Shapeshifters sat in a semicircle with Valentine facing them and the tiny, wizened old Vroon at his left hand. The Pontifex ran his glance down the group, from the site-boss Kaastisiik at one end to the paleographer Vo-Simiifon on the other. They looked back at him calmly, almost indifferently, these seven rubbery-faced slope-eyed Piurivars, as he told them of the things he had seen this day, the cemetery and the shattered pyramid and the shrine beneath it, and the alcove where Huukaminaan's severed head had been so carefully placed by his murderer. "There was, wouldn't you say, a certain formal aspect to the murder?" Valentine said. "The cutting of the body into pieces? The carrying of the head down to the shrine? The placement in the alcove of offerings?" His gaze fastened on Thiuurinen, the ceramics expert, a lithe, diminutive Metamorph woman with lovely jade-green skin. "What's your reading on that?" he asked her.

Her expression was wholly impassive. "As a ceramicist I have no opinion at all."

"I don't want your opinion as a ceramicist, just as a member of the expedition. A colleague of Dr. Huukaminaan's. Does it seem to you that putting the head there meant that some kind of offering was being made?"

"It is only conjecture that those alcoves were places of offering," said Thiuurinen primly. "I am not in a position to speculate."

Nor would she. Nor would any of them. Not Kaastisiik, not Vo-Simiifon, not the stratigrapher Pamikuuk, not Hieekraad, the custodian of material artifacts, nor Driismiil, the architectural specialist, nor Klelliin, the authority on Piurivar paleo-technology, nor Viitaal-Twuu, the specialist in metallurgy.

Politely, mildly, firmly, unshakably, they brushed aside Valentine's hypotheses about ritual murder. Was the gruesome dismemberment of Dr. Huukaminaan a hearkening-back to the funereal practices of ancient Velalisier? Was the placing of his head in that alcove likely to have been any kind of propitiation of some supernatural being? Was there anything in Piurivar tradition that might countenance killing someone in that particular fashion? They could not say. They would not say. Nor, when he inquired as to whether their late colleague might have had an enemy here at the site, did they provide him with any information.

And they merely gave him the Piurivar equivalent of a shrug when he wondered out loud whether there could have been some struggle over the discovery of a valuable artifact that might have led to Huukaminaan's murder; or even a quarrel of a more abstract kind, a fierce disagreement over the findings or goals of the expedition. Nobody showed any sign of outrage at his implication that one of them might have killed old Huukaminaan over such a matter. They behaved as though the whole notion of doing such a thing were beyond their comprehension, a concept too alien even to consider.

During the course of the interview Valentine took the opportunity to aim at least one direct question at each of them. But the result was always the same. They were unhelpful without seeming particularly evasive. They were unforthcoming without appearing unusually sly or secretive. There was nothing overtly suspicious about their refusal to cooperate. They seemed to be precisely what they claimed to be: scientists, studious scholars devoted to uncovering the buried mysteries of their race's remote past who knew nothing at all about the mystery that had erupted right here in their midst. He did not feel himself to be in the presence of murderers here.

And yet... and yet...

They were Shapeshifters.

He was the Pontifex, the emperor of the race that had conquered them, the successor across eight thousand years of the half-legendary soldier-king Lord Stiamot who had deprived them of their independence for all time. Mild and scholarly though they might be, these eight Piurivars before him surely could not help but feel anger, on some level of their souls, toward their human masters.

They had no reason to cooperate with him. They would not see themselves under any obligation to tell him the truth. And -- was this only his innate and inescapable racial prejudices speaking, Valentine wondered? -- intuition told him to take nothing at face value among these people. Could he really trust the impression of apparent innocence that they gave? Was it possible ever for a human to read the things that lay hidden behind a Metamorph's cool impenetrable features?

"What do you think?" he asked Deliamber, when the seven Shapeshifters had gone. "Murderers or not?"

"Probably not," the Vroon replied. "Not these. Too soft, too citified. But they were holding something back. I'm certain of that."

"You felt it too, then?"

"Beyond any doubt. What I sensed, your majesty -- do you know what the Vroon word 'hsirthiir' means?"

"Not really."

"It isn't easy to translate. But it has to do with questioning someone who doesn't in-tend to tell you any lies but isn't necessarily going to tell you the truth either, unless you know exactly how to call it forth. You pick up a powerful perception that there's an important layer of meaning hidden somewhere beneath the surface of what you're being told, but that you won't be allowed to elicit that hidden meaning unless you ask precisely the right question to unlock it. Which means, essentially, that you already have to know the information that you're looking for before you can ask the ques-tion that would reveal it. It's a very frustrating sensation, hsirthiir: almost painful, in fact. It is like hitting one's beak against a stone wall. I felt myself placed in a state of hsirthiir just now. Evidently so did you, your majesty."

"Evidently I did," said Valentine.

There was one more visit to make, though. It had been a long day and a terrible weariness was coming over Valentine now. But he felt some inner need to cover all the basic territory in a single sweep; and so, once darkness had fallen, he asked Magadone Sambisa to conduct him to the village of the Metamorph laborers.

She was unhappy about that. "We don't usually like to intrude on them after they've finished their day's work and gone back there, your majesty."

"You don't usually have murders here, either. Or visits from the Pontifex. I'd rather speak with them tonight than disrupt tomorrow's digging, if you don't mind."

Deliamber accompanied him once again. At her own insistence, so did Lisamon Hultin. Tunigorn was too tired to go -- his hike through the ruins at midday had done him in -- and Mirigant was feeling feverish from a touch of sunstroke; but formidable old Duke Nascimonte readily agreed to ride with the Pontifex, despite his great age. The final member of the party was Aariisim, the Metamorph member of Valentine's security staff, whom Valentine brought with him not so much for protection -- Lisamon Hultin would look after that -- as for the hsirthir problem.

Aarisiim, turncoat though he once had been, seemed to Valentine to be as trustworthy as any Piurivar was likely to be. He had risked his own life to betray his master Faraataa to Valentine in the time of the Rebellion, when he had felt that Faraataa had gone beyond all decency by threatening to slay the Metamorph queen. He could be helpful now perhaps, detecting things that eluded even Deliamber's powerful perceptions.

The laborers' village was a gaggle of meager wickerwork huts outside the central sector of the dig. In its flimsy, makeshift look it reminded Valentine of Ilirivoyne, the Shape-shifter capital in the jungle of Zimroel, which he had visited so many years before. But this place was even sadder and more disheartening than Ilirivoyne. There, at least, the Metamorphs had had an abundance of tall, straight saplings and jungle vines with which to build their ramshackle huts, whereas the only construction materials available to them here were the gnarled and twisted desert shrubs that dotted the Velalisier plain. And so their huts were miserable little things, dismally warped and contorted.

They had had advance word, somehow, that the Pontifex was coming. Valentine found them arrayed in groups of eight or ten in front of their shacks, clearly waiting for his ar-rival. They were a pitiful, starved-looking bunch, gaunt and shabby and ragged, very dif-ferent from the urbane and cultivated Metamorphs of Magadone Sambisa's archaelogi-cal team. Valentine wondered where they found the strength to do the digging that was required of them in this inhospitable climate.

As the Pontifex came into view, they shuffled forward to meet him, quickly sur-rounding him and the rest of his party in a way that caused Lisamon Hultin to hiss sharply and put her hand to the hilt of her vibration-sword.

But they did not appear to mean any harm. They clustered excitedly around him and to his amazement offered homage in the most obsequious way, jostling among themselves for a chance to kiss the hem of his tunic, kneeling in the sand before him, even prostrating themselves.

"No," Valentine cried, dismayed. "This isn't necessary. It isn't right." Already Maga-done Sambisa was ordering them brusquely to get back, and Lisamon Hultin and Nascimonte were shoving the ones closest to Valentine away from him. The giant-ess was doing it calmly, unhurriedly, efficiently, but Nascimonte was prodding them more truculently, with real detestation apparent in his fiery eyes.

Others came pressing forward as fast as the first wave retreated, though, pushing in upon him in frantic determination.

So eager were these weary, toil-worn people to show their obeisance to the Pontifex in fact, that he could not help regarding their enthusiasm as blatantly false, an ostentatious overdoing of whatever might have been appropriate. How likely was it, he wondered, that any group of Piurivars, however lowly and simple, would feel great unalloyed joy at the sight of the Pontifex of Majipoor? Or would, of their own accord, stage such a spontaneous demonstration of delight?

Some, men and women both, were even allowing themselves to mimic the forms of the visitors by way of compliment, so that half-a-dozen blurry, distorted Valentines stood before him, and a couple of Nascimontes, and a grotesque, half-sized imitation of Lisamon Hultin. Valentine had experienced that peculiar kind of honor before, in his Ilirivoyne visit, and he had found it disturbing and even chilling then. It distressed him again now. Let them shift shapes if they wished -- they had that capacity to use as they pleased -- but there was something almost sinister about this appropriation of the visages of their visitors. And the jostling began to grow even wilder and more frenzied. Despite himself, Valentine started to feel some alarm.

There were more than a hundred villagers, and the visitors numbered only a handful. There could be real trouble if things got out of control.

Alone in his grand royal tent at last after the interminable exertions of the busy day, he found himself missing Carabella with surprising intensity: that small and sinewy woman who had shared his destiny almost from the beginning of the strange time when he had found himself at Pidruid, at the other continent's edge, bereft of all memory, all knowledge of self. It was she, loving him only for himself, all unknowing that he was in fact a Colonel in baffled exile from his true identity, who had helped him join the juggling troupe of Zalzan Kavol; and gradually their lives had merged; and when he had commenced his astounding return to the heights of power, she had followed him to the summit of the world.

He wished she were with him now. To sit beside him, to talk with him as they always talked before bedtime. To go over with him the twisting ramifications of all that had been set before him this day. To help him make sense out of the tangled mysteries this dead city posed for him. And simply to be with him. But Carabella had not followed him here to Velalisier. It was a foolish waste of his time, she had argued, for him to go in person to investigate this murder. Send Tunigorn; send Mirigant; send Sleet; send any one of a number of high Pontifical officials. But why go yourself?

"Because I must," Valentine had replied. "Because I've made myself responsible for integrating the Metamorphs into the life of this world. The excavations at Velalisier are an essential part of that enterprise. And the murder of the old archaeologist leads me to think that conspirators are trying to interfere with those excavations."

"This is very far-fetched," said Carabella, then.

"And if it is, so be it. But you know how I long for a chance to free myself of the Labyrinth, if only for a week or two. So I will go to Velalisier."

"And I will not. I loathe that place, Valentine. It's a horrid place of death and destruction. I've seen it twice, and its charm isn't growing on me. If you go, you'll go without me."

"I mean to go, Carabella."

"Go, then. If you must." And she kissed him on the tip of the nose, for they were not in the custom of quarreling, or even of disagreeing greatly. But when he went, it was indeed without her. She was in their royal chambers in the Labyrinth tonight, and he was here, in his grand but solitary tent, in this parched and broken city of ancient ghosts.

They came to him that night in his dreams, those ghosts.

They came to him with such intensity that he thought he was having a sending -- a lucid and purposeful direct communication in the form of a dream.

But this was like no sending he had ever had. Hardly had he closed his eyes but he found himself wandering in his sleep among the cracked and splintered buildings of dead Velalisier. Eerie ghost-light, mystery-light, came dancing up out of every shattered stone. The city glowed lime-green and lemon-yellow, pulsating with inner luminescence. Glowing faces, ghost-faces, grinned mockingly at him out of the air. The sun itself swirled and leaped in wild loops across the sky.

A dark hole leading into the ground lay open before him, and unquestioningly he entered it, descending a long flight of massive lichen-encrusted stone steps with archaic twining runes carved in them. Every movement was arduous for him. Though he was going steadily lower, the effort was like that of climbing. Struggling all the way, he made his way ever deeper, but he felt constantly as though he were traveling upward against a powerful pull, ascending some inverted pyramid, not a slender one like those above ground in this city, but one of unthinkable mass and diameter. He imagined himself to be fighting his way up the side of a mountain; but it was a mountain that pointed downward, deep into the world's bowels. And the path was carrying him down, he knew, into some labyrinth far more frightful than the one in which he dwelled in daily life.

The whirling ghost-faces flashed dizzyingly by him and went spinning away. Cackling laughter floated backward to him out of the darkness. The air was moist and hot and rank. The pull of gravity was oppressive. As he descended, traveling through level after endless level, momentary flares of dizzying yellow light showed him caverns twisting away from him on all sides, radiating outward at incomprehensible angles that were both concave and convex.

And now there was sudden, numbing brightness. The throbbing fire of an underground sun streamed upward toward him from the depths ahead of him, a harsh, menacing glare.

Valentine found himself drawn helplessly toward that terrible light; and then, without perceptible transition, he was no longer underground at all, but out in the vastness of Velalisier Plain, standing atop one of the great platforms of blue stone known as the Tables of the Gods.

There was a long knife in his hand, a curving scimitar that flashed like lightning in the brilliance of the noon sun.

And as he looked out across the plain, he saw a mighty procession coming toward him from the east, from the direction of the distant sea. Thousands of people, hundreds of thousands, like an army of ants on the march. No, two armies; for the marchers were divided into two great, parallel columns. Valentine could see at the end of each column far off near the horizon two enormous wooden wagons mounted on titanic wheels. Great hawsers were fastened to them, and the marchers, with mighty groaning tugs, were hauling the wagons slowly forward, a foot or two with each pull, into the center of the city.

Atop each of the wagons a colossal water-king lay trussed, a sea-dragon of monstrous size. The great creatures were glaring furiously at their captors but were unable, even with a sea-dragon's prodigious strength, to free themselves from their bonds, strain as they might. And with each tug on the hawsers, the wagons bearing them carried them closer to the twin platforms called the Tables of the Gods.

The place of the sacrifice.

The place where the terrible madness of the Defilement was to happen. Where Valentine the Pontifex of Majipoor waited with the long, gleaming blade in his hand.

"Majesty? Majesty?"

Valentine blinked and came groggily awake. A Shapeshifter stood above him, extremely tall and greatly attenuated of form, his eyes so sharply slanted and narrowed that it seemed at first glance that he had none at all. Valentine began to jump up in alarm; and then, recognizing the intruder after a moment as Aarisiim, he relaxed.

"You cried out," the Metamorph said. "I was on my way to you to tell you some strange news I have learned, and when I was outside your tent I heard your voice. Are you all right, your majesty?"

"A dream, only. A very nasty dream." Which still lingered disagreeably at the edges of his mind. Valentine shivered and tried to shake himself free of its grasp. "What time is it, Aarisiim?"

"The Hour of the Haigus, majesty."

Past the middle of the night, that was. Well along toward dawn. Valentine forced himself the rest of the way into wakefulness. Eyes fully open now, he stared up into the practically featureless face. "There's news, you say? What news?"

The Metamorph's color deepened from pale green to a rich chartreuse, and his eye-slits fluttered swiftly three or four times. "I have had a conversation this night with one of the archaeologists, the woman Hieekraad, she who keeps the records of the discovered artifacts. The foreman of the diggers brought her to me, the man Vathiimeraak, from the village. He and this Hieekraad are lovers, it seems."

Valentine stirred impatiently. "Get to the point, Aarisiim."

"I approach it, sir. The woman Hieekraad, it seems, has revealed things to the man Vathiimeraak about the excavations that a mere foreman might otherwise not have known. He has told those things to me this evening."

"Well?"

"They have been lying to us, majesty -- all the archaeologists, the whole pack of them, deliberately concealing something important. Something quite important, a major discovery. Vathiimeraak, when he learned from this Hieekraad that we had been deceived in this way, made the woman come with him to me, and compelled her to reveal the whole story to me."

"Go on."

"It was this," said Aarisiim. He paused a moment, swaying a little as though he were about to plunge into a fathomless abyss. "Dr. Huukaminaan, two weeks before he died, uncovered a burial site that had never been detected before. This was in an otherwise desolate region out at the western edge of the city. Magadone Sambisa was with him. It was a post-abandonment site, dating from the historic era. From a time not long after Lord Stiamot, actually."

"But how could that be?" said Valentine, frowning. "Completely aside from the little matter that there was a curse on this place and no Piurivar would have dared to set foot in it after it was destroyed, there weren't any Piurivars living on this continent at that time anyway. Stiamot had sent them all into the reservations on Zimroel. You know that very well, Aarisiim. Something's wrong here."

"This was not a Piurivar burial, your majesty."

"What?"

"It was the tomb of a human," Aarisiim said. "The tomb of a Pontifex, according to the woman Hieekraad."

Valentine would not have been more surprised if Aarisiim had set off an explosive charge. "A Pontifex?" he repeated numbly. "The tomb of a Pontifex, here in Velalisier?"

"So did this Hieekraad say. A definite identification. The symbols on the wall of the tomb -- the Labyrinth sign, and other things of that sort, the ceremonial objects found lying next to the body, inscriptions, everything indicated that this was a Pontifex's grave, thousands of years old. So she said; and I think she was telling the truth. Vathiimeraak was standing over her, scowling, as she spoke. She was too frightened of him to have uttered any falsehoods just then."

Valentine rose and paced fiercely about the tent. "By the Divine, Aarisiim! If this is true, it's something that should have been brought to my attention as soon as it came to light. Or at least mentioned to me upon my arrival here. The tomb of some ancient Pontifex, and they hide it from me? Unbelievable. Unbelievable!"

"It was Magadone Sambisa herself who ordered that all news of the discovery was to be suppressed. There would be no public announcement whatsoever. Not even the diggers were told what had been uncovered. It was to be a secret known to the archaeologists of the dig only."

"This according to Hieekraad also?"

"Yes, majesty. She said that Magadone Sambisa gave those orders the very day the tomb was found. This Hieekraad furthermore told me that Dr. Huukaminaan disagreed strenuously with Magadone Sambisa's decision, that indeed they had a major quarrel over it. But in the end he gave in. And when the murder happened, and word came that you were going to visit Velalisier, Magadone Sambisa called a meeting of the staff and reiterated that nothing was to be said to you about it. Everyone involved with the dig was specifically told to keep all knowledge of it from you."

"Absolutely incredible," Valentine muttered.

Earnestly Aarissim said, "You must protect the woman Hieekraad, majesty, as you investigate this thing. She will be in great trouble if Magadone Sambisa learns that she's the one who let the story of the tomb get out."

"Hieekraad's not the only one who's going to be in trouble," Valentine said. He slipped from his nightclothes and started to dress.

"One more thing, majesty. The khivanivod -- Torkkinuuminaad? He's at the tomb site right now. That's where he went to make his prayer retreat. I have this information from the foreman Vathiimeraak."

"Splendid," Valentine said. His head was whirling. "The village khivanivod mumbling Piurivar prayers in the tomb of a Pontifex! Beautiful! Wonderful! Get me Magadone Sambisa right away, Aarisiim."

"Majesty, the hour is very early, and -- "

"Did you hear me, Aarisiim?"

"Majesty," said the Shapeshifter, more subserviently this time. He bowed deeply and went out to fetch Magadone Sambisa.

"An ancient Pontifex's tomb, Magadone Sambisa, and no announcement is made? An ancient Pontifex's tomb, and when the current Pontifex comes to inspect your dig, you go out of your way to keep him from learning about it? This is all extremely difficult for me to believe, let me assure you."

Dawn was still an hour away. Magadone Sambisa, called from her bed for this interview, looked even paler and more haggard than she had yesterday, and now there might have been a glint of fear in her eyes as well. But for all that, she still was capable of summoning some of the unrelenting strength that had propelled her to the forefront of her profession; there was even a steely touch of defiance in her voice as she said, "Who told you about this tomb, your majesty?"

Valentine ignored the sally. "It was at your order, was it, that the story was suppressed?"

"Yes."

"Over Dr. Huukaminaan's strong objections, so I understand."

Now fury flashed across her features. "They've told you everything, haven't they? Who was it? Who?"

"Let me remind you, lady, that I am the one asking the questions here. It's true then, that Huukaminaan disagreed with you about concealing the discovery?"

"Yes." In a very small voice.

"Why was that?"

"He saw it as a crime against the truth," Magadone Sambisa said, still speaking very quietly now. "You have to understand, majesty, that Dr. Huukaminaan was utterly dedicated to his work. Which was, as it is for us all, the recovery of the lost aspects of our past through rigorous application of formal archaeological disciplines. He was totally committed to this, a true and pure scientist."

"Whereas you are not committed quite so totally?"

Magadone Sambisa reddened and glanced shamefacedly to one side. "I admit that my actions may make it seem that way. But sometimes even the pursuit of truth has to give way, at least for a time, before tactical realities. Surely you, a Pontifex, would not deny that. And I had reasons, reasons that seemed valid enough to me, for not wanting to let news of this tomb reach the public. Dr. Huukaminaan didn't agree with my position; and he and I battled long and hard over it. It was the only occasion in our time as co-leaders of this expedition that we disagreed over anything."

"And finally it became necessary, then, for you to have him murdered? Because he yielded to you only grudgingly, and you weren't sure he really would keep quiet?"

"Majesty!" It was a cry of almost inexpressible shock.

"A motive for the killing can be seen there. Isn't that so?"

She looked stunned. She waved her arms helplessly about, the palms of her hands turned outward in appeal. A long moment passed before she could bring herself to speak. But she had recovered much of her composure when she did.

"Majesty, what you have just suggested is greatly offensive to me. I am guilty of hiding the tomb discovery, yes. But I swear to you that I had nothing to do with Dr. Huukaminaan's death. I can't possibly tell you how much I admired that man. We had our professional differences, but -- " She shook her head. She looked drained. Very quietly she said, "I didn't kill him. I have no idea who did."

Valentine chose to accept that, for now. It was hard for him to believe that she was merely play-acting her distress.

"Very well, Magadone Sambisa. But now tell me why you decided to conceal the finding of that tomb."

"I would have to to tell you first an old Piurivar legend, a tale out of their mythology, one that I heard from the khivanivod Torkkinuuminaad on the day that we found the tomb."

"Must you?"

"I must, yes."

Valentine sighed. "Go ahead, then."

Magadone Sambisa moistened her lips and drew a deep breath.

"There once was a Pontifex, so the story goes," she said, "who lived in the years soon after the conquest of the Piurivars by Lord Stiamot. This Pontifex had fought in the War of the Conquest himself when he was a young man, and had had charge over a camp of Piurivar prisoners, and had listened to some of their campfire tales. Among which was the story of the Defilement at Velalisier -- the sacrifice by the Final King of the two sea-dragons, and the destruction of the city that followed it. They told him also of the broken Seventh Pyramid, and of the shrine beneath it, the Shrine of the Downfall, as they called it. In which, they said, certain artifacts dating from the day of the Defilement had been buried -- artifacts that would, when properly used, grant their wielder god-like power over all the forces of space and time. This story stayed with him, and many years later when he had become Pontifex he came to Velalisier with the intention of locating the shrine of the Seventh Pyramid, the Shrine of the Downfall, and opening it."

"For the purpose of bringing forth these magical artifacts, and using them to gain god-like power over the forces of space and time?"

"Exactly," said Magadone Sambisa.

"I think I see where this is heading."

"Perhaps you do, majesty. We are told that he went to the site of the shattered pyramid. He drove a tunnel into the ground; he came upon the stone passageway that leads to the wall of the shrine. He found the wall and made preparations for breaking through it."

"But the seventh shrine, you told me, is intact. Since the time of the abandonment of the city no one has ever entered it. Or so you believe."

"No one ever has. I'm sure of that."

"This Pontifex, then -- ?"

"Was just at the moment of breaching the shrine wall when a Piurivar who had hidden himself in the tunnel overnight rose up out of the darkness and put a sword through his heart."

"Wait a moment," said Valentine. Exasperation began to stir in him. "A Piurivar popped out of nowhere and killed him, you say? A Piurivar? I've just gone through this same thing with Aarisiim. Not only weren't there any Piurivars anywhere in Alhanroel at that time, because Stiamot had locked them all up in reservations over in Zimroel, but there was supposed to be a curse on this place that would have prevented members of their race from going near it."

"Except for the guardians of the shrine, who were exempted from the curse," said Magadone Sambisa.

"Guardians?" Valentine said. "What guardians? I've never heard anything about Piurivar guardians here."

"Nor had I, until Torkkinuuminaad told me this story. But at the time of the city's destruction and abandonment, evidently, a decision was made to post a small band of watchmen here, so that nobody would be able to break into the seventh shrine and gain access to whatever's was in there. And that guard force remained on duty here throughout the centuries. There were still guardians here when the Pontifex came to loot the shrine. One of them tucked himself away in the tunnel and killed the Pontifex just as he was about to chop through the wall."

"And his people buried him here? Why in the world would they do that?"

Magadone Sambisa smiled. "To hush things up, of course. Consider, majesty: A Pontifex comes to Velalisier in search of forbidden mystical knowledge, and is assassinated by a Piurivar who has been sneaking around undetected in the supposedly abandoned city. If word of that got around, it would make everyone look bad."

"I suppose that it would."

"The Pontifical officials certainly wouldn't have wanted to let it be known that their master had been struck down right under their noses. Nor would they be eager to advertise the story of the secret shrine, which might lead others to come here looking for it, too. And surely they'd never want anyone to know that the Pontifex had died at the hand of a Piurivar, something that could reopen all the wounds of the War of the Conquest and perhaps touch off some very nasty reprisals."

"And so they covered everything up," said Valentine.

"Exactly. They dug a tomb off in a remote corner of the ruins and buried the Pontifex in it with some sort of appropriate ritual, and went back to the Labyrinth with the news that his majesty had very suddenly been stricken down at the ruins by an unknown disease and it had seemed unwise to bring his body back from Velalisier for the usual kind of state funeral. Ghorban was his name. There's an inscription in the tomb that names him. Ghorban Pontifex, three Pontifexes after Stiamot. He really existed. I did research in the House of Records. You'll see him listed there"

"I'm not familiar with the name."

"No. He's not exactly one of the famous ones. But who can remember them all anyway? Hundreds and hundreds of them, across all those thousands of years. Ghorban was Pontifex only a short while, and the only event of any importance that occurred during his reign was something that was carefully obliterated from the records. I'm speaking of his visit to Velalisier."

Valentine nodded. He had paused by the great screen outside the Labyrinth's House of Records often enough, and many times had stared at that long list of his predecessors, marveling at the names of all-but-forgotten monarchs, Meyk and Spurifon and Heslaine and Kandibal and dozens more who must have been great men in their day, but their day was thousands of years in the past. No doubt there was a Ghorban on the list if Magadone Sambisa said there had been: one who had reigned in regal grandeur for a time as the Colonel Lord Ghorban atop Castle Mount, and then had succeeded to the Pontificate in the fullness of his years, and for some reason had paid a visit to this accursed city of Velalisier, where he died, and was buried, and fell into oblivion.

"A curious tale," Valentine said. "But what is there in it that would have made you want to suppress the discovery of this Ghorban's tomb?"

"The same thing that made those ancient Pontifical officials suppress the real circumstances of his death," replied Magadone Sambisa. "You surely know that most ordinary people already are sufficiently afraid of this city. The horrible story of the Defilement, the curse, all the talk of ghosts lurking in the ruins, the general spookiness of the place -- well, you know what people are like, your majesty. How timid they can be in the face of the unknown. And I was afraid that if the Ghorban story came out -- the secret shrine, the search for mysterious magical lore by some obscure ancient Pontifex, the murder of that Pontifex by a Piurivar -- there'd be such public revulsion against the whole idea of excavating Velalisier that the dig would be shut down. I didn't want that to happen. That's all it was, your majesty. I was trying to preserve my own job, I suppose. Nothing more than that."

It was a humiliating confession. Her tone, which had been vigorous enough during the telling of the tale, now was flat, weary, almost lifeless. To Valentine it had the sound of complete sincerity.

"And Dr. Huukaminaan didn't agree with you that revealing the discovery of the tomb could be a threat to the continuation of your work here?"

"He saw the risk. He didn't care. For him the truth came first and foremost, always. If public opinion forced the dig to be shut down, and nobody worked here again for fifty or a hundred or five hundred years, that was all right with him. His integrity wouldn't permit hiding a startling piece of history like that, not for any reason. So we had a big battle and finally I pushed him into giving in. You've seen how stubborn I can be. But I didn't kill him. If I had wanted to kill anybody, it wouldn't have been Dr. Huukaminaan. It would have been the khivanivod, who actually does want the dig shut down."

"He does? You said he and Huukaminaan worked hand-in-glove."

"In general, yes. As I told you yesterday, there was one area where he and Huukaminaan diverged: the issue of opening the shrine. Huukaminaan and I, you know, were planning to open it as soon as we could arrange for you and Lord Hissune to be present at the work. But the khivanivod was passionately opposed. The rest of our work here was acceptable to him, but not that. The Shrine of the Downfall, he kept saying, is the holy of holies, the most sacred Piurivar place."

"He might just have a point there," Valentine said.

"You also don't think we should look inside that shrine?"

"I think that there are certain important Piurivar leaders who might very much not want that to happen."

"But the Danipiur herself has given us permission to work here! Not only that, but she and all the rest of the Piurivar leaders understand that we've come here to restore the city -- that we hope to undo as much as we can of the harm that thousands of years of neglect have caused. They have no quarrel with that. But just to be completely certain that our work would give no offense to the Piurivar community, we all agreed that the expedition would consist of equal numbers of Piurivar and non-Piurivar archaeologists, and that Dr. Huukaminaan and I would share the leadership on a co-equal basis."

"Although you turned out to be somewhat more co-equal than he was when there happened to be a significant disagreement between the two of you, didn't you?"

"In that one instance of the Ghorban tomb, yes," said Magadone Sambisa, looking just a little out of countenance. "But only that one. He and I were in complete agreement at all times on everything else. On the issue of opening the shrine, for example."

"A decision which the khivanivod then vetoed."

"The khivanivod has no power to veto anything, majesty. The understanding we had was that any Piurivar who objected to some aspect of our work on religious grounds could appeal to the Danipiur, who would then adjudicate the matter in consultation with you and Lord Hissune."

"Yes. I wrote that decree myself, actually."

Valentine closed his eyes a moment and pressed the tips of his fingers against them. He should have realized, he told himself, that problems like these would inevitably crop up. This city had too much tragic history. Terrible things had happened here. The mysterious aura of Piurivar sorcery still hovered over the place, thousands of years after its destruction.

He had hoped to dispel some of that aura by sending in these scientists. Instead he had only enmeshed himself in its dark folds.

After a time he looked up and said, "I understand from Aarisiim that where your khivanivod has gone to make his spiritual retreat is in fact the Ghorban tomb that you've taken such pains to hide from me, and that he's there at this very moment. Is that true?"

"I believe it is."

The Pontifex walked to the tent entrance and peered outside. The first bronze streaks of the desert dawn were arching across the great vault of the sky.

"Last night," he said, "I asked you to send messengers out looking for him, and you said that you would. You didn't, of course, tell me that you knew where he was. But since you do know, get your messengers moving. I want to speak with him first thing this morning."

"And if he refuses to come, your majesty?"

"Then have him brought."

The khivanivod Torkkinuuminaad was every bit as disagreeable as Magadone Sambisa had led Valentine to expect, although the fact that it had been necessary for Valentine's security people to threaten to drag him bodily from the Ghorban tomb must not have improved his temper. Lisamon Hultin was the one who had ordered him out of there, heedless of his threats and curses. Piurivar witcheries and spells held little dread for her, and she let him know that if he didn't go to Valentine more or less willingly on his own two feet, she would carry him to the Pontifex herself.

The Shapeshifter shaman was an ancient, emaciated man, naked but for some wisps of dried grass around his waist and a nasty-looking amulet, fashioned of interwoven insect legs and other such things, that dangled from a frayed cord about his neck. He was so old that his green skin had faded to a faint gray, and his slitted eyes, bright with rage, glared balefully at Valentine out of sagging folds of rubbery skin.

Valentine began on a conciliatory note. "I ask your pardon for interrupting your meditations but certain urgent matters must be dealt with before I return to the Labyrinth, and your presence was needed for that."

Torkkinuuminaad said nothing.

Valentine proceeded regardless. "For one thing, a serious crime has been committed in the archaeological zone. The killing of Dr. Huukaminaan is an offense not only against justice but against knowledge itself. I'm here to see that the murderer is identified and punished."

"What does this have to do with me?" asked the khivanivod, glowering sullenly. "If there has been a murder, you should find the murderer and punish him, yes, if that is what you feel you must do. But why must a servant of the Gods That Are be compelled by force to break off his sacred communion like this? Because the Pontifex of Majipoor commands it?" Torkkinuuminaad laughed harshly. "The Pontifex! Why should the commands of the Pontifex mean anything to me? I serve only the Gods That Are."

"You also serve the Danipiur," said Valentine in a calm, quiet tone. "And the Danipiur and I are colleagues in the government of Majipoor." He indicated Magadone Sambisa and the other archaeologists, both human and Metamorph, who stood nearby. "These people are at work in Velalisier this day because the Danipiur has granted her permission for them to be here. You yourself are here at the Danipiur's request, I believe, to serve as spiritual counsellor for those of your people who are involved in the work."

"I am here because the Gods That Are require me to be here, and for no other reason."

"Be that as it may, your Pontifex stands before you, and he has questions to ask you, and you will answer."

The shaman's only response was a sour glare.

"A shrine has been discovered near the ruins of the Seventh Pyramid," Valentine went on. "I understand that the late Dr. Huukaminaan intended to open that shrine. You had strong objections to that, am I correct?"

"You are."

"Objections on what grounds?"

"That the shrine is a sacred place not to be disturbed by profane hands."

"How can there be a sacred place," asked Valentine, "in a city that had a curse pronounced on it?"

"The shrine is sacred nevertheless," the khivanivod said obdurately.

"Even though no one knows what may be inside it?"

"I know what is inside it," said the khivanivod.

"You? How?"

"I am the guardian of the shrine. The knowledge is handed down from guardian to guardian."

Valentine felt a chill traveling along his spine. "Ah," he said. "The guardian. Of the shrine." He was silent a moment. "As the officially designated successor, I suppose, of the guardian who murdered a Pontifex here once thousands of years ago. The place where you were found praying just now, so I've been told, was the tomb of that very Pontifex. Is that so?"

"It is."

"In that case," said Valentine, allowing a little smile to appear at the corners of his mouth, "I need to ask my guards to keep very careful watch on you. Because the next thing I'm going to do, my friend, is to instruct Magadone Sambisa and her people to proceed at once with the opening of the seventh shrine. And I see now that that might place me in some danger at your hands."

Torkkinuuminaad looked astounded. Abruptly the Metamorph shaman began to go through a whole repertoire of violent changes of form, contracting and elongating wildly, the borders of his body blurring and recomposing with bewildering speed.

But the archaeologists too, both the human ones and the two Ghayrogs and the little tight-knit group of Shapeshifters, were staring at Valentine as though he had just said something beyond all comprehension. Even Tunigorn and Mirigant and Nascimonte were flabbergasted. Tunigorn turned to Mirigant and said something, to which Mirigant replied only with a shrug, and Nascimonte, standing near them, shrugged also in complete bafflement.

Magadone Sambisa said in hoarse choking tones, "Majesty? Do you mean that? I thought you said only a little while ago that the best thing would be to leave the shrine unopened!"

"I said that? I?" Valentine shook his head. "Oh, no. No. How long will it take you to get started on the job?"

"Why... let me see..." He heard her murmur, "The recording devices, the lighting equipment, the masonry drills... " She grew quiet, as if counting additional things off in her mind. Then she said, "We could be ready to begin in half an hour."

"Good. Let's get going, then."

"No! This will not be!" cried Torkkinuumaad, a wild screech of rage.

"It will," said Valentine. "And you'll be there to watch it. As will I." He beckoned toward Lisamon Hultin. "Speak with him, Lisamon. Tell him in a persuasive way that it'll be much better for him if he remains calm."

Magadone Sambisa said, wonderingly, "Are you serious about all this, Pontifex?"

"Oh, yes. Yes. Very serious indeed."

The day seemed a hundred hours long.

Opening any sealed site for the first time would ordinarily have been a painstaking process. But this one was so important, so freighted with symbolic significance, so potentially explosive in its political implications, that every task was done with triple care.

Valentine himself waited at surface level during the early stages of the work. What they were doing down there had all been explained to him: running cables for illumination and ventilating pipes for the excavators, carefully checking with sonic probes to make sure that opening the shrine wall would not cause the ceiling of the vault to collapse, sonic testing of the interior of the shrine itself to see if there was anything important immediately behind the wall that might be imperiled by the drilling operation.

All that took hours. Finally they were ready to start cutting into the wall.

"Would you like to watch, majesty?" Magadone Sambisa asked.

Despite the ventilation equipment, Valentine found it hard work to breathe inside the tunnel. The air had been hot and stale enough on his earlier visit; but now, with all these people crowded into it, it was thin, feeble stuff, and he had to strain his lungs to keep from growing dizzy.

The close-packed archaeologists parted ranks to let him come forward. Bright lights cast a brilliant glare on the white stone facade of the shrine. Five people were gathered there, three Piurivars, two humans. The actual drilling seemed to be the responsibility of the burly foreman Vaathimeraak. Kaastisiik, the Piurivar archaeologist who was the site boss, was assisting. Just behind them was Driismiil, the Piurivar architectural expert, and a human woman named Shimrayne Gelvoin, who also was an architect, evidently. Magadone Sambisa stood to the rear, quietly issuing orders.

They were peeling the wall back stone by stone. Already an area of the facade perhaps three feet square had been cleared just above the row of offering-alcoves. Behind it lay rough brickwork, no more than one course thick. Vaathimeraak, muttering to himself in Piurivar as he worked, now was chiseling away at one of the bricks. It came loose in a crumbling mass, revealing an inner wall made of the same fine black stone slabs as the tunnel wall itself.

A long pause, now, while the several layers of the wall were measured and photographed. Then Vaathimerak resumed the inward probing. Valentine was at the edge of queasiness in this foul, acrid atmosphere, but he forced it back.

Vaathimeraak cut deeper, halting to allow Kaastisiik to remove some broken pieces of the black stone. The two architects came forward and inspected the opening, conferring first with each other, then with Magadone Sambisa; and then Vaathimeraak stepped toward the breach once again with his drilling tool.

"We need a torch," Magadone Sambisa said suddenly. "Give me a torch, someone!"

A hand-torch was passed up the line from the crowd in the rear of the tunnel. Magadone Sambisa thrust it into the opening, peered, gasped.

"Majesty? Majesty, would you come and look?"

By that single shaft of light Valentine made out a large, rectangular room which appeared to be completely empty except for a large square block of dark stone. It was very much like the glossy block of black opal, streaked with veins of scarlet ruby, from which the glorious Confalume Throne at the castle of the Colonel had been carved.

There were things lying on that block. But what they were was impossible to tell at this distance.

"How long will it take to make an opening big enough for someone to enter the room?" Valentine asked.

"Three hours, maybe."

"Do it in two. I'll wait aboveground. You call me when the opening is made. Be certain that no one enters it before me."

"You have my word, majesty."

Even the dry desert air was a delight after an hour or so of breathing the dank stuff below. Valentine could see by the lengthening shadows creeping across the deep sockets of the distant dunes that the afternoon was well along. Tunigorn, Mirigant, and Nascimonte were pacing about amidst the rubble of the fallen pyramid. The Vroon Deliamber stood a little distance apart.

"Well?" Tunigorn asked.

"They've got a little bit of the wall open. There's something inside, but we don't know what yet."

"Treasure?" Tunigorn asked with a lascivious grin. "Mounds of emeralds and diamonds and jade?"

"Yes," said Valentine. "All that and more. Treasure. An enormous treasure, Tunigorn." He chuckled and turned away. "Do you have any wine with you, Nascimonte?"

"As ever, my friend. A fine Muldemar vintage."

He handed his flask to the Pontifex, who drank deep, not pausing to savor the bouquet at all, guzzling as though the wine were water.

The shadows deepened. One of the lesser moons crept into the margin of the sky.

"Majesty? Would you come below?"

It was the archaeologist Vo-Siimifon. Valentine followed him into the tunnel.

The opening in the wall was large enough now to admit one person. Magadone Sambisa, her hand trembling, handed Valentine the torch.

"I must ask you, your majesty, to touch nothing, to make no disturbance whatever. We will not deny you the privilege of first entry, but you must bear in mind that this is a scientific enterprise. We have to record everything just as we find it before anything, however trivial, can be moved."

"I understand," said Valentine.

He stepped carefully over the section of the wall below the opening and clambered in.

The shrine's floor was of some smooth glistening stone, perhaps rosy quartz. A fine layer of dust covered it. No one has walked across this floor for twenty thousand years, Valentine thought. No human foot has ever come in contact with it at all.

He approached the broad block of black stone in the center of the room and turned the torch full on it. Yes, a single, dark mass of ruby-streaked opal, just like the Confalume throne. Atop it, with only the faintest tracery of dust concealing its brilliance, lay a flat sheet of gold, engraved with intricate Piurivar glyphs and inlaid with cabochons of what looked like beryl and carnelian and lapis lazuli. Two long, slender objects that could have been daggers carved from some white stone lay precisely in the center of the gold sheet, side by side.

Valentine felt a tremor of the deepest awe. He knew what those two things were.

"Majesty? Majesty?" Magadone Sambisa called. "Tell us what you see! Tell us, please!"

But Valentine did not reply. It was as though Magadone Sambisa had not spoken. He was deep in memory, traveling back eight years to the climactic hour of the War of the Rebellion.

He had, in that hour, held in his hand a dagger-like thing much like these two, and had felt the strange coolness of it, a coolness that gave a hint of a fiery core within, and had heard a complex far-off music emanating from it into his mind, a turbulent rush of dizzying sound.

It had been the tooth of a sea-dragon that he had been grasping then. Some mystery within that tooth had placed his mind in communion with the mind of the mighty water-king Maazmoorn, a dragon of the distant Inner Sea. And with the aid of the mind of Maazmoorn had Valentine Pontifex reached across the world to strike down the unrepentent rebel Faraataa and bring that sorry uprising to an end.

Whose teeth were these now?

He thought he knew. This was the Shrine of the Downfall, the Place of the Defilement. Not far from here, long ago, two water-kings had been brought from the sea to be sacrificed on platforms of blue stone. That was no myth. It had actually happened. Valentine had no doubt of that, for the sea-dragon Mazmoorn had shown it to him with the full communion of his mind, in a manner that admitted of no question. He knew their names, even: one was the water-king Niznorn and the other the water-king Domsitor. Was this tooth here Niznorn's, and this one Domsitor's?

Twenty thousand years.

"Majesty? Majesty?"

"One moment," Valentine said, speaking as though from halfway around the world.

He picked up the left-hand tooth. Grasped it tightly. Hissed as its fiery chill stung the palm of his hand. Closed his eyes, allowed his mind to be pervaded by its magic. Felt his spirit beginning to soar outward and outward and outward, toward some waiting dragon of the sea -- Maazmoorn again, for all he could know, or perhaps some other one of the giants who swam in those waters out there -- while all the time he heard the sounding bells, the tolling music of that sea-dragon's mind.

And was granted a vision of the ancient sacrifice of the two water-kings, the event known as the Defilement.

He already knew, from Mazmoorn in that meeting of minds years ago, that that traditional name was a misnomer. There had been no defilement whatever. It had been a voluntary sacrifice; it had been the formal acceptance by the sea-dragons of the power of That Which Is, which is the highest of all the forces of the universe.

The water-kings had given themselves gladly to those Piurivars of long-ago Velalisier to be slain. The slayers themselves had understood what they were doing, perhaps, but the simple Piurivars of the outlying provinces had not; and so those simpler Piurivars had called it a Defilement, and had put the Final King of Velalisier to death and smashed the Seventh Pyramid and then had wrecked all the rest of this great capital, and had laid a curse on the city forever. But the shrine of these teeth they had not dared to touch.

Valentine, holding the tooth, beheld the sacrifice once more. Not with the bound sea-dragons writhing in fury as they were brought to the knife, the way he had seen it in his nightmare of the previous night. No. He saw it now as a serene and holy ceremony, a benign yielding up of the living flesh. And as the knives flashed, as the great sea-creatures died, as their dark flesh was carried to the pyres for burning, a resounding wave of triumphant harmony went rolling out to the boundaries of the universe.

He put the tooth down and picked up the other one. Grasped. Felt. Surrendered himself to its power.

This time the music was more discordant. The vision that came to him was that of some unknown man of middle years, garbed in a rich costume of antique design, clothing befitting to a Pontifex. He was moving cautiously by the smoky light of a flickering torch down the very passageway outside this room where Magadone Sambisa and her archaeologists now clustered. Valentine watched that Pontifex of long ago approaching the white, unsullied wall of the shrine. Saw him press the flat of his hand against it, pushing as though he hoped to penetrate it by his own strength alone. Turning from it, then beckoning to workmen with picks and spades, indicating that they should start hacking their way through it.

And a figure uncoiling out of the darkness, a Shapeshifter, long and lean and grim-faced, taking one great step forward and in a swift unstoppable lunge driving a knife upward and inward beneath the heart of the man in the brocaded Pontifical robes.

"Majesty, I beg you!"

Magadone Sambisa's voice, ripe with anguish.

"Yes," said Valentine, in the distant tone of one who has been lost in a dream. "I'm coming."

He had had enough visions for the moment. He set the torch down on the floor, aiming it toward the opening in the wall to light his way. Carefully he picked up the two dragon-teeth -- letting them rest easily on the palms of his hands, taking care not to touch them so tightly as to activate their powers, for he did not want now to open his mind to them -- and made his way back out of the shrine.

Magadone Sambisa stared at him in horror. "I asked you, your majesty, not to touch the objects in the vault, not to cause any disturbance to --"

"Yes. I know that. You will pardon me for what I have done."

It was not a request.

The archaeologists melted back out of his way as he strode through their midst, heading for the exit to the upper world. Every eye was turned to the things that rested on Valentine's upturned hands.

"Bring the khivanivod to me here," he said quietly to Aariisiim. The light of day was nearly gone now, and the ruins were taking on the greater mysteriousness that came over them by night, when moonlight's cool gleam danced across the shattered city's ancient stones.

The Shapeshifter went rushing away. Valentine had not wanted the khivanivod anywhere near the shrine while the opening of the wall was taking place; and so, over his violent objections, Tork-kanuuminaad had been bundled off to the archaeologists' headquarters in the custody of some of Valentine's security people. The two immense woolly Skandars brought him forth now, holding him by the arms.

Anger and hatred were bubbling up from the shaman like black gas rising from a churning marsh. And, staring into that jagged green wedge of a face, Valentine had a powerful sense of the ancient magic of this world, of mysteries reaching toward him out of the timeless misty Majipoor dawn, when Shapeshifters had moved alone and unhindered through this great planet of marvels and splendors.

The Pontifex held the two sea-dragon teeth aloft.

"Do you know what these are, Torkkanuuminaad?"

The rubbery eye-folds drew back. The narrow eyes were yellow with rage. "You have committed the most terrible of all sacrileges, and you will die in the most terrible of agonies."

"So you do know what they are, eh?"

"They are the holiest of holies! You must return them to the shrine at once!"

"Why did you have Dr. Huukaminaan killed, Torkkanuuminaad?"

The khivanivod's only answer was an even more furiously defiant glare.

He would kill me with his magic, if he could, thought Valentine. And why not? I know what I represent to Turkkanuuminaad. For I am Majipoor's emperor and therefore I am Majipoor itself, and if one thrust would send us all to our doom I would strike that thrust.

Yes. Valentine was in his own person the embodiment of the Enemy: of those who had come out of the sky and taken the world away from the Piurivars, who had built their own gigantic sprawling cities over virgin forests and glades, had intruded themselves by the billions into the fragile fabric of the Piurivars' trembling web of life. And so Torkkanuuminad would kill him, if he could, and by killing the Pontifex kill, by the symbolism of magic, all of human-dominated Majipoor.

But magic can be fought with magic, Valentine thought.

"Yes, look at me," he told the shaman. "Look right into my eyes, Torkkanuuminaad."

And let his fingers close tightly about the two talismans he had taken from the shrine.

The double force of the teeth struck into Valentine with a staggering impact as he closed the mental circuit. He felt the full range of the sensations all at once, not simply doubled, but multiplied many times over. He held himself upright nevertheless; he focused his concentration with the keenest intensity; he aimed his mind directly at that of the khivanivod.

Looked. Entered. Penetrated the khivanivod's memories and quickly found what he was seeking.

Midnight darkness. A sliver of moonlight. The sky ablaze with stars. The billowing tent of the archaeologists. Someone coming out of it, a Piurivar, very thin, moving with the caution of age.

Dr. Huukaminaan, surely.

A slender figure stands in the road, waiting: another Metamorph, also old, just as gaunt, raggedly and strangely dressed.

The khivanivod, that one is. Viewing himself in his own mind's eye.

Shadowy figures moving about behind him, five, six, seven of them. Shapeshifters all. Villagers, from the looks of them. The old archaeologist does not appear to see them. He speaks with the khivanivod; the shaman gestures, points. There is a discussion of some sort. Dr. Huukaminaan shakes his head. More pointing. More discussion. Gestures of agreement. Everything seems to be resolved.

As Valentine watches, the khivanivod and Huukaminaan start off together down the road that leads to the heart of the ruins.

The villagers, now, emerging from the shadows that have concealed them. Surrounding the old man; seizing him; covering his mouth to keep him from crying out. The khivanivod approaches him.

The khivanivod has a knife.

Valentine did not need to see the rest of the scene. Did not want to see that monstrous ceremony of dismemberment at the stone platform, nor the weird ritual afterward in the excavation leading to the Shrine of the Downfall, the placing of the dead man's head in that alcove.

He released his grasp on the two sea-dragon teeth and set them down with great care beside him on the ground.

"Now," he said to the khivanivod, whose expression had changed from one of barely controllable wrath to one that might almost have been resignation. "There's no need for further pretending here, I think. Why did you kill Dr. Huukaminaan?"

"Because he would have opened the shrine." The khivanivod's tone was completely flat, no emotion in it at all.

"Yes. Of course. But Magadone Sambisa also was in favor of opening it. Why not kill her instead?"

"He was one of us, and a traitor," said Torkkanuuminaad. "She did not matter. And he was more dangerous to our cause. We know that she might have been prevented from opening the shrine if we objected strongly enough. But nothing would stop him."

"The shrine was opened anyway, though," Valentine said.

"Yes, but only because you came here. Otherwise the excavations would have been closed down. The outcry over Huukaminaan's death would demonstrate to the whole world that the curse of this place still had power. You came and you opened the shrine; the curse will strike you just as it struck the Pontifex Ghorban long ago."

"There is no curse," Valentine said calmly. "This is a city that has seen much tragedy, but there is no curse, only misunderstanding piled on misunderstanding."

"The Defilement -- "

"There was no Defilement either, only a sacrifice. The destruction of the city by the people of the provinces was a vast mistake."

"So you understand our history better than we do, Pontifex?"

"Yes," said Valentine. "Yes. I do." He turned away from the shaman and said, glancing toward the village foreman, "Vathiimeraak, there are murderers living in your settlement. I know who they are. Go to the village now and announce to everyone that if the guilty ones will come forward and confess their crime, they'll be pardoned after they undergo a full cleansing of their souls."

Turning next to Lisamon Hultin, he said, "As for the khivanivod, I want him handed over to the Danipiur's officials to be tried in her own courts. This falls within her area of responsibility. And then -- "

"Majesty!" someone called. "Beware!"

Valentine swung around. The Skandar guards had stepped back from the khivanivod and were staring at their own trembling hands as though they had been burned in a fiery furnace. Torkinuuminaad, freed of their grasp, thrust his face up into Valentine's. His expression was one of diabolical intensity.

"Pontifex!" he whispered. "Look at me, Pontifex! Look at me!"

Taken by surprise, Valentine had no way of defending himself. Already a strange numbness had come over him. The dragon-teeth went tumbling from his helpless hands. Torkinuuminaad was shifting shape now, running through a series of grotesque changes at a frenzied rate, so that he appeared to have a dozen arms and legs at once, and half-a-dozen bodies; and he was casting some sort of spell. Valentine was caught in it like a moth in a spider's cunningly woven strands. The air seemed thick and blurred before him, and a wind had come up out of nowhere. Valentine stood perplexed, trying to force his gaze away from the khivanivod's fiery eyes, but he could not. Nor could he find the strength to reach down and seize hold of the two dragon-teeth that lay at his feet. He stood as though frozen, muddled, dazed, tottering. There was a burning sensation in his breast and it was a struggle simply to draw breath.

There seemed to be phantoms all around him. A dozen Shapeshifters -- a hundred, a thousand. Grimacing faces. Glowering eyes. Teeth, claws, knives. A horde of wildly cavorting assassins surrounded him, dancing, bobbing, gyrating, hissing, mocking him, calling his name derisively. He was lost in a whirlwind of ancient sorceries.

"Lisamon?" Valentine cried, baffled. "Deliamber? Help me. Help -- " But he was not sure that the words had actually escaped his lips.

Then he saw that his guardians had indeed perceived his danger. Deliamber, the first to react, came rushing forward, flinging his own many tentacles up hastily in a counter-spell, a set of gesticulations and thrusts of mental force intended to neutralize whatever was emanating from Torkkinuuminaad. And then, as the little Vroon began to wrap the Piurivar shaman in his web of Vroonish wizardry, Vathi-imeraak advanced on Torkinuuminaad from the opposite side, boldly seizing the shaman in complete indifference to his spells, forcing him down to the ground, bending him until his forehead was pressing against the soil at Valentine's feet.

Valentine felt the grip of the shaman's wizardry beginning to ebb, then easing further, finally losing its last remaining hold on his soul. The contact between Torkinuuminaad's mind and his gave way with an almost audible snap.

Vathiimeraak released the khivanivod and stepped back. Lisamon Hultin now came to the shaman's side and stood menacingly over him. But the episode was over. The shaman remained where he was, absolutely still now, staring at the ground, scowling bitterly in defeat.

"Thank you," Valentine said simply to Deliamber and Vathiimeraak. And, with a dismissive gesture, "Take him away."

Lisamon Hultin threw Torkinuuminaad over her shoulder like a sack of calimbots and went striding off down the road.

A long, stunned silence followed. Magadone Sambisa broke it, finally. In a hushed voice she said, "Your majesty, are you all right?"

He answered only with a nod.

"And the excavations," she said anxiously, after another moment. "What will happen to them? Will they continue?"

"Why not?" Valentine replied. "There's still much work to be done." He took a step or two away from her. He touched his hands to his chest, to his throat. He could still almost feel the pressure of those relentless invisible hands.

Magadone Sambisa was not finished with him, though.

"And these?" she asked, indicating the sea-dragon teeth. She spoke more aggressively now, taking charge of things once again, beginning to recover her vigor and poise. "If I may have them now, majesty -- "

Angrily Valentine said, "Take them, yes. But put them back in the shrine. And then seal up the hole you made today."

The archaeologist stared at him as though he had turned into a Piurivar himself. With a note of undisguised asperity in her voice she said, "What, your majesty? What? Dr. Huuka-minaan died for those teeth! Finding that shrine was the pinnacle of his work. If we seal it up now -- "

"Dr. Huukaminaan was the perfect scientist," Valentine said, not troubling to conceal his great weariness now. "His love of the truth cost him his life. Your own love of truth, I think, is less than perfect, and therefore you will obey me in this."

"I beg you, majesty -- "

"No. Enough begging. I don't pretend to be a scientist at all, but I understand my own responsibilities. Some things should remain buried. These teeth are not things for us to handle and study and put on display at a museum. The shrine is a holy place to the Piurivars, even if they don't understand its own holiness. It's a sad business for us all that it ever was uncovered. The dig itself can continue, in other parts of the city. But put these back. Seal that shrine and stay away from it. Understood?"

She looked at him numbly, and nodded.

"Good. Good."

The full descent of darkness was settling upon the desert now. Valentine could feel the myriad ghosts of Velalisier hovering around him. It seemed that bony fingers were plucking at his tunic, that eerie, whispering voices were murmuring perilous magics in his ears.

Most heartily he yearned to be quit of these ruins. He had had all he cared to have of them for one lifetime.

To Tunigorn he said, "Come, old friend, give the orders. Make things ready for our immediate departure.

"Now, Valentine? At this late hour?"

"Now, Tunigorn. Now." He smiled. "Do you know, this place has made the Labyrinth seem almost appealing to me! I feel a great desire to return to its familiar comforts. Come, get everything organized for leaving. We've been here quite long enough."

The End.

CONCEPTUAL ART

JUL   2007

variations:

Deliamber Vroon